It is Finished

Why you can quit religion and trust in Jesus

Blaise Foret

DEDICATION

This book is dedicated to all of my friends and followers on Facebook, Twitter, Instagram and YouTube. I wouldn't be doing what I am doing without all of you. I genuinely love you guys and I'm so encouraged by your continued perseverance in the message of pure grace and love. Heaven is watching and the family is awakening. Cheers to another big year of waking up the world to the love of God!

CONTENTS

ACKNOWLEDGMENTS

Tony Seigh for your continued encouragement to write this book and for sticking with me through all of the transition these past two years.

Austin Roberts for being a true friend and being fearless in challenging the religious norms with a sincere and loving heart. JB4L.

My amazing parents who have always supported me in every endeavor God put in my heart. You two are gold. Dad, thanks for putting up with my zealot years when I didn't have ears to hear what you told me about the simple *good news*.

My siblings for being amazing. Love you all more than I can express.

My financial partners. Without you guys, I would still be serving espresso in Kansas City.

Phyllis for your love and support. You helped make this possible.

Carole and **Lauren** for your tireless editing. You took me back to English class ☺

The boys from the never-ending group text. Your hourly encouragement is always a wonderful distraction.

The Barista's at Crema in Nashville for letting me sit in your coffee shop for 8 hours a day on my computer. I know I looked like a spoiled college kid without a job, but I was really writing a book ☺ You guys rock and your coffee is amazing.

All of the amazing people I've met in Nashville over the last 5 months. You all have changed my life and made me a better person. I'm in love with you guys and with this city!

And of course, **Jesus**. You're my wonderful obsession.

INTRODUCTION

Have you ever asked the questions that get you in trouble at Church? You know, the ones that Pastors usually answer with a scowl on their faces saying,

"Because the Bible says so, young man!"

Those questions that come into the mind of every *good Christian kid* when he or she finally steps into their first college class or sits in their room alone while all their friends go out and *party*.

Questions like these…

If God is good, then why does everything seem so bad?

If God is actually good, then why is He blamed for all the bad?

If God is so wonderful, then why do most Christians seem so miserable?

How can I really be sure that I am "saved" or that anyone is actually "saved"?

Did the cross actually work?

Was Christ's coming just a cosmic failure since most pastors say that the majority of the world is going to burn in hell?

What is the point of all this?

What is the POINT?!?!?

I've asked all those questions, and I've gotten into some trouble for it. But I've also come to a few conclusions that have dramatically changed the way I live life and love the people around me.

For most of you, the fact that you even picked up this book tells me that you probably fit into one of these categories:

-*Normative Christian* looking for a little clarity on how to be a *better* Christian.

-*Failure Christian* just trying to find *something* that might help keep you from losing your faith altogether.

-*Zealous Christian* looking for a *deeper* relationship with God.

-Dedicated *Guardian of Christian Orthodoxy* ready to underline and highlight all of my *errors*.

-*Former Christian* who once believed in the *God of the Bible* but due to life circumstances and intellectual contradictions has taken on more of an *Agnostic* position.

-*Average Joe* looking for more purpose in life.

Or maybe you're just bored, sitting in a bookstore and picked up this random book to read.

For whatever reason that you picked up this book…

this book

is

for you.

JOIN ME IN MY JOURNEY OF DISCOVERY

This is my invitation for you to join me in a deep, yet enjoyable conversation about God and His purpose for humanity—you included.

Since I grew up in the *Christian Church,* there were a lot of things I thought I *already knew* about God, Jesus, and *the Bible*. Many of you might find yourself in the same boat.

If so, this book is for you.

Some of you might be 100% sure there is nothing more you could be told about God that you *don't already know*. You may have read the Bible hundreds of times and heard thousands of *sermonettes* at your local church or small group.

If that's you, then you might wonder, *"How could a book claim to give me some new information about God?"*

Well, I won't claim to give you *brand new information* about God. But I will probably say some things you have never heard before. Not because these ideas themselves are *new*. Dear God, by all means, they are the oldest truths in the book (literally). But somewhere along the way, we have definitely lost these gems; we started to swallow a different view of God that seems to be more like *Zeus* and a different *gospel* that emphasizes what *we must do* rather than what *He has done*!

If you are looking for a theological masterpiece, then please give this book to a local college student and go pick up a book by *St. Athanasius* or *Robert F. Capon*.

But for you folks who crave simplicity *with some depth*, I believe you will walk away from this book with a greater sense of understanding God's love for you, your eternal and secure destiny as His kid, and what the work of Jesus Christ on the cross means for the *entire world*.

I am honored that you would join me on this wonderful journey of discovering the God whom I have come to know as *Completely Good* and *Completely Kind.*

So please, grab a coffee (or your favorite drink), sit back, take a deep breath, and let's dive in.

CHAPTER 1
JESUS AND THE DESTRUCTION OF RELIGION
The God Who Challenged the System

Humanity longs to worship something bigger than ourselves.

We all long to see something or someone that will take us to our true origin.

Kind of like a super-hero. Someone to save us, teach us our origin, and show us how to become like the *gods*.

Religion is actually all about mankind's desire to worship *their gods* and mankind's journey to *become like their gods*.

Every now and then I find myself in conversations where genuine folks want to defend the validity of religion and present it as a helpful thing. They always say,

"Blaise, religion is bad. But true religion is good. Remember? That Bible verse in James says so."

Sure, I'll give you that.

Sounds like a great deal.

True religion.

Well, we shall see…

Actually, the word *religion* comes from the Greek word *"thrēskeia"*. One of the meanings of the word is *the fear of the gods.*

Really? The *fear of the gods?*

Sounds fun to me.

Another meaning of the word is *the practice of external ceremonies and worship.*

It seems like the inside of the heart is more important than the external motions of *worship* that someone may or may not perform. Even so, what we *do* does matter, in a sense. It matters because we were made to love—and love always has an expression.

That is the entire point of the *little bible verse* about *true religion.* I can almost imagine James speaking tongue-in-cheek,

*"Ladies and gents, I know that we come from a very religious culture. Our entire history is full of external ceremonies and rituals that we love so dearly. Since you love religion so much, I won't take that from you…I'll just redefine it. If you want religion and external rituals, then how about you **externally** take care of the poor? Instead of continuing with Old Covenant shadows and ceremonies, take time to give someone a hug and a few bucks when you pass them on your way to the Temple. Now that's true religion."*

Jesus did not come to establish a new *external religious system.*

He came to the woman at the well and told her,

*"I know that you Samaritans say worship services should happen at this mountain and that the Jews say that worship services should happen at a different mountain. But let me tell you a little secret. The whole earth is full of the glory, and **true worship** is done by those who recognize that*

heaven is not far away. It's right here! In fact, not only is heaven here and now, but God is here and now. You're in Him and He's in you. (See John 4, Luke 17:21 and John 17).

How in the world are we supposed to package a religion like that? God living inside of us? Rushing rivers of God-life right smack-dab in the middle of our bellies?

This can't be controlled.

That's the point of religion anyway — **control.**

Always keeping people on the rat race of *trying to reach God.*

Jesus came to declare that those days were over and a **new day** had begun.

*"On that day you will **realize** that **I am in my Father and you are in me and I am in you,"*** (see John 14:20).

Years ago, I worked with a ministry that did a lot of teaching and preaching. One day I met with one of the Pastors from that church and asked him questions about some doctrine that the church preached. I began sharing with him what I had been learning by listening to other teachers *outside of that ministry.*

"Hmmm…"

He looked concerned.

*"You should really limit yourself to listening to teachings from our church and steer clear of listening to too many teachers who are not from **our stream**,"* he said with a concerned tone.

I began to realize that religion builds machines that feed on man-power. If people stop believing the doctrines that fuel their voluntary service to the machine then…

the machine…

will…

run…

out…

of…

steam…

When the machine begins losing power, the leaders panic and put the pressure on the people. Usually it's through fear and guilt.

Those other people are *wrong*. Their teaching is *dangerous*.

They are *in error.*

They are *off.*

Why? Because if *they* don't line up with *us,* then they might steal *you* from *us.*

It seems like Christianity is really missing the point when we have to keep our machines running by limiting what our people are hearing. It's religious control and it's dangerous. I don't think this guy had any clue what he was doing, nor do I think his motives were wrong. But that is the problem; the control runs so deep in our religious culture that we don't even realize when we are operating in that vein.

If anyone ever tells you to *only listen to their teachings,* then head for the frickin' hills, son.

The gospel never comes to control or manipulate through the fear. God is confident in the fact that *love always wins.* Religion is afraid of losing control. God enjoys giving people freedom to think for themselves and to be persuaded by love.

So many have considered themselves to be *guardians of the truth* to the point of *calling out* and *rebuking* people for thinking or believing differently than their own church or religious organization. I appreciate conversations and exhortations when it has to do with growing in truth, but when it comes to controlling what others believe, then it is misguided *at best* and can become very damaging.

History tells us the same thing.

Much of the *persecution and martyrdom* of the Christian Church has come from those who declared themselves to be of the *orthodox position* and opposed those who began thinking for themselves and challenging the system.

Regardless of whether or not they were *right* or *wrong* in their so-called *heretical positions,* they did not deserve physical abuse or death for asking questions.

The problem, as I see it, is that those who desperately desire to *keep the truth* become so dedicated to their version of *truth* that they forget to actually love people. That's why, historically, *heretics have been killed.*

Does that concern anyone else?

The *biblical people* killed the *unbiblical people?*

So…

*…the people who believed the **truth** were supposedly inspired to kill people and not love people?*

Orthodoxy has a pretty rough history: all the way from the time when the most biblical Pharisees had Jesus crucified to the 1500's when the Catholic Church wanted to have Luther killed.

I honestly wonder if it weren't for the secular laws we have in place today if many pastors, teachers, and other academics out there would still be alive.

Not that we shouldn't seek truth. But we've got to see a bigger picture than just *guarding the truth*. Love is the greatest expression of truth and without love, our so-called *truth* is actually a bunch of funny business.

STAIRWAY TO HEAVEN

There's something innately placed in mankind that knows we were made for greatness, pleasure, and eternal life; we were made for **God**. Ever since the beginning of time, mankind has always tried to create a stairway back to heaven.

Every time we try and find a pathway to our divinity God always frustrates the plan. Since the fall of Adam, we have continued to try to work our way back to our heavenly dwelling.

Genesis 11 talks about a group of people who remembered what they were made for and started building a tower to the sky. Some think it was a monument and others think they were actually trying to climb their way back to heaven. Either way, they knew they were made for greatness.

God saw their self-effort and decided to frustrate their religious plans by giving them all different languages. They all quickly dispersed from their plans when they realized the Chinese tractor operator could no longer communicate with the project director who spoke pig-latin.

At the end of the day, these guys were trying to gain a heavenly status through their self-effort. When all along, friendship with God would have made it clear to them that they already had a heavenly status.

There are many different definitions of religion, but I'll go with this one: *working to gain what is freely given or trying to become what we already are.*

The Jews had this same problem. For thousands of years they studied the law and sought to keep it perfectly, and many of them actually thought they did. There was absolutely nothing wrong with the law.

The law was good. But the law was never God's original intention for mankind.

It was more of an in-between stage for a disobedient people who forgot who they were and who their Father was.

Through the law, God met man on our own terms.

We didn't want relationship, we wanted rules.

We didn't want mercy, we wanted judgment.

So God met us on our terms.

God's original intention has always been a *love relationship* not *forced obedience.*

When God created Adam and Eve, He didn't set up a bunch of rules for them to follow. He said, "Be fruitful and multiply. And don't eat from the Tree of the Knowledge of Good and Evil." Now that's a good deal!

*"Guys, go enjoy one another and enjoy the garden I gave you! Oh, and don't sit around wondering about right and wrong. That's actually **none of your concern.**"*

CHOPPING DOWN THAT OLE' TREE

The tree of the knowledge of good and evil is exactly that, trying to figure out what is good and what is evil. God doesn't want us messing around with that kind of thinking. He has something so much more enjoyable for us! Jesus called it *life and life abundantly.*

Religion has created an industry based on figuring out what's right and wrong.

We were never supposed to spend our time thinking about rights and wrongs. We were *made right with God* when we were created. God's one command was that we *would remember who we really are and where we come from.* When we dug into that malnourishing meal from the ole' tree of religion, we believed the lie of the enemy.

What was that lie? That we have to *become like God.*

As though somewhere along the way we were no longer *like Him…*

But that was the lie: that God didn't *really* make us in His image and likeness.

"Let us make man in **Our image** and in **Our likeness.**" –God (Genesis 2)

The enemy came to Eve and accused God of withholding something from mankind and making us less than perfect. Then, of course, he convinced them that the only way to become like God was to have their *eyes opened* to light and darkness, good and evil, right, and wrong.

Once they ate of that tree, they realized that they were basically in a nudist colony.

This wasn't "wrong" before. But when sin entered the picture, their lack of clothing became *nakedness*. That's why God asked them the question, *"Who told you that you were naked?"*

The glory that clothed them before the fall was still there, but their eyes had been blinded to the truth. God saw perfection; they saw *nakedness*. God saw beauty; they saw blemishes.

Relax, I'm not trying to promote nudist colonies.

What I am saying is that God has seen us as a *perfect reflection of His image from the very beginning*. There was nothing we could do to add to that and nothing we had to do to gain acceptance from Him. We were covered by His glory until we were *told* that we were naked and incomplete.

Adam and Eve chose to eat the fruit of that tree and have their eyes opened to a knowledge that they were never meant to carry. God's original intent for mankind was that we would live life and live it abundantly.

His desire for us is that we would

be good

and

see good

all around us.

He never wanted us to have to live trying to figure out right and wrong, good and evil. "Don't taste, don't touch, etc. etc." (see Colossians 2). These commands come from the tree of religion. We were never made for that tree. We were made for the **Tree of Life.**

That was the *only tree we were made to eat from*. It's time to chop down that ole' tree of "right and wrong" and "good and evil." It's time to eat from the Tree of Life—Jesus Himself. This Tree is full of life and light.

In that tree there is no death and no darkness. Eating from the Tree of Life only produces more life and more love. This is what true *living* is really all about.

JESUS FRUSTRATES THE RELIGIONIST

Jesus is such a funny dude.

Seriously, as soon as you think you have Him figured out, He does something or says something that is completely opposite of what you had concluded about Him. This is what happened to the Pharisees when He showed up.

Can you imagine? The Pharisees had spent their lives studying the character of God and the attributes of the coming Messiah. They knew when He was coming and they knew what He would do. They created systems and structures to explain and contain Him.

But when Jesus actually came on the scene, these guys found out that He didn't fit in with their systems and structures at all. In fact, He broke their rules and ended up spending the majority of His time with the screw-ups and the folks that the system had condemned as *unclean*.

Unlike the religionist, Jesus didn't come to nit-pick at their lifestyles. Instead, He came to remind them that they were heavenly offspring, loved by a Dad who was willing to die for them.

The Religionists had studied the law so intently that they even came up with new laws that helped explain what God must've *really meant* when He gave the law. They created laws on top of laws and commands within commands.

The law said, *"Rest on the Sabbath."*

The Religionist said, *"Don't do anything on the Sabbath." (see Luke 14)*

The law said, *"Be generous and give a tithe."*

The Religionist said, *"Even if your family is struggling and needs that money to survive, you should still give us your money and let your family starve." (see Matthew 15)*

Jesus came and rebuked the religious folk reminding them that the whole point of life was *love*. Man wasn't made for law; the law was made for man. But the religious mind always takes what was meant to serve us and turns it into a *god* – imagining that by serving this *law*, they are somehow pleasing God.

Jesus came on the scene and told the poor widow that she was amazing for giving all that she had when the Pharisees sneered at her for not giving *enough*. The way that a religious person judges others is a good clue about the way they judge themselves. The work is never *finished* and what is given is never *enough*.

Jesus' disciples did some "harvesting" on the Sabbath to grab a bite to eat and Jesus didn't care at all. The Pharisees came and rebuked Jesus for not rebuking His boys over this matter. Jesus told them that even in the Old Covenant David broke the law and it was actually

no... big... deal.

Again, the Pharisees showed up to get Jesus in trouble when He fixed a dude's hand on the Sabbath. Totally healed the bro. *"But wait, it was on the Sabbath and I'm sure that healing took **some kind of effort**, Jesus."*

I can only imagine Jesus looking at those Pharisees sarcastically saying,

*"Guys, if you were sitting at home on the Sabbath in your lazy-boy and you got a text from your friend saying that someone stole your car, then I guarantee that you'd be outa' that chair faster than you can say, 'Save us, Lord!' If you'd take care of your property like that, then how much more should I take care of the human race every single day of the week! Love isn't **work** for me; it's as easy as breathing. And my Dad and I never stop loving the human race... you shouldn't either." (Luke 14 paraphrase)*

JESUS WANTS YOU TO FAIL

Jesus didn't care to keep the rules, and He wasn't impressed with those who claimed to keep all of them. In fact, when people boasted in their flawless rule-keeping, **Jesus made up new rules for them.**

"Oh, you're good at rules? Cool. I'm the guy who made them, so I can make a few more for ya since you enjoy them so much."

Check out the story of Jesus talking to this rich guy who asked him how to get eternal life:

"(Jesus answered,) You can get to heaven if you keep the commandments." "Which ones?" the man asked. And Jesus replied, "Don't kill, don't commit adultery, don't steal, don't lie, honor your father and mother, and love your neighbor as yourself!" "I've always obeyed every one of them," the youth replied. "What else must I do?"

Jesus told him, "If you want to be perfect, go and sell everything you

have and give the money to the poor, and you will have treasure in heaven; and come, follow me." But when the young man heard this, he went away sadly, for he was very rich." Matthew 19:16-22 (Living Bible)

Did you catch that? Jesus just **made up a brand new commandment for this guy**. Can you imagine looking at God and saying, *"Yep, I did all that stuff that You said. What else you got for me, Lord?"*

So, Jesus speaks with the man on his own terms, *"Well, little buddy, since you've been such a good boy, I'll give you one more challenge. Sell all your stuff, give away the money, and come follow Me. Then you'll be saved! Got it?"*

The man walked away discouraged because he finally heard a command that He couldn't keep.

Another one bites the dust.

This religionist couldn't handle the command. Thankfully, the story doesn't end there. If we can take another look through the *lens of grace and love* then, we might find that it actually ends on a positive note.

The disciples, being sharp as they were, spoke up and said, *"Jesus! Wow, that was intense. Man, you really told that guy. He just couldn't hack it, I guess. Couldn't handle the heat. Nope, not like us. We left everything to follow You. Yep, everything. So...we're good, right?*

Right?

Ummm...Jesus?"

Jesus answers, *"Guys, it is really tough for a rich man to be saved. In fact, it's easier to park a mac-truck in a compact car parking space than for a rich man to be saved."*

[GASP!]

[GULP…]

"THEN WHO CAN BE SAVED, JESUS?!?!?!?!?," cried the disciples.

(That's the whole point, right? **Who can be saved?**)

Finally, Jesus could get to the punch line.

*"Well, if it's up to you guys and your rule-keeping religious efforts and your good-boy to-do list… ummmm, pretty much, **no one**. In fact, **I want you to fail**… I want you to fail at religion…"*

*"BUT, if it's up to Me, then **absolutely nothing is impossible and the doors are open to <u>everyone</u>.**"*

The point of this story was not that we would all feel bad for the rich man and think, *"Wow, Christianity is only for the spiritually tough guys who will be poor and broke enough for Jesus."*

Sounds really spiritual, but **it's not the gospel**.

Actually, the guy who had the most hope of being saved in this story is the guy who actually walked away realizing that he couldn't save himself.

Did you get that? The rich dude **finally** had come to the *end of himself.* Jesus couldn't have set him up any better for the gospel.

I can only imagine the guy thinking, *"Gosh, I've done everything perfect my whole life. I just dropped the ball. I'm not perfect anymore? I guess I can't be saved. **I quit!**"*

And of course, Jesus is probably thinking, *"Finally, he **failed**. Now He can actually realize that He never needed to try in the first place. I am his **origin**. I am his **perfection**. And I am his **salvation**."*

RETIRING

The best thing you can do is give up.

Yes, *give up.*

Quit.

Don't even turn in a 2-week's notice. The business is going downhill already and you are no longer needed as an employee. In fact, it went out of business about two thousand years ago when Jesus showed up.

Retire from the broken down religious establishment and come to a place of rest. Start living off of the benefits of retirement—the finished work of the cross.

Retire?

Quit?

Rest?

REALLY???

Sounds dangerous.

Too good to be true…and possibly even heretical.

Check out what the writer of Hebrews has to say about this:

Therefore, let us fear if, while a promise remains of entering His rest, any one of you may seem to have come short of it. 2 For indeed we have had good news preached to us, just as they also; but the word they heard did not profit them, because it was not united by faith in those who heard. 3 For we who have believed enter that rest, just as He has said, "As I swore in My wrath, They shall not enter My rest," although His works

were finished from the foundation of the world.
Hebrews 4:1-3 (NASB)

I'll try to break this down **quickly**. We've got a lot more fun stuff to get to....

The Hebrews were coming out of a system of law and into the New Covenant. The writer of Hebrews was doing his best to help transition them out of that old system and fully into the message of grace and truth through Jesus.

So he uses the examples that they knew, **Jewish history.**

Moses led the people out of slavery, but that entire generation died in the wilderness (except Joshua and Caleb). *The Promised Land* was the land of rest for the Hebrews. But only a few folks ended up coming to that land of *rest*. The reason they didn't make it?

It wasn't because they didn't work hard enough, pray hard enough, fast enough, or give enough. **None of that mattered.**

The reason they missed out on the *rest* that God promised them was because they simply didn't *believe God.*

Believing God has to do with *letting go* and *trusting Him.* Simple as that. You don't have to work up belief. Just simple trust will do.

But in order to trust Him, you have to lose trust in yourself and let go of your own abilities to achieve **goodness and perfection.**

The Israelites weren't willing to **retire from their efforts** and **trust in God's promise,** so they didn't enter into *rest.* Literally, for them that meant wandering around the wilderness until they died. Kinda sucks.

The writer of Hebrews is warning the Hebrews of the 1st Century who witnessed the death and resurrection of Christ of the same fate. Not in an actual wilderness, but in a spiritual one. It was though they were wandering around for years trying to re-accomplish what Christ had already accomplished, still trying to make sacrifices on behalf of their sins. But Christ had already come and His sacrifice was their complete redemption.

The Hebrews who were willing to listen to the gospel decided to let go of the old system that was passing away and embrace the New Covenant that was freely given.

By calling this covenant "new," he has made the first one obsolete; and what is obsolete and outdated will soon disappear.

Hebrews 8:13 (NIV)

It was a good thing they did, because about 10 years later, the Roman army came marching into Jerusalem and destroyed the old system altogether.

Jesus had come and *fulfilled* mankind's need for *sacrifice*. But many of the Jews of the day refused to embrace Him and continued with their sacrifices that were only a shadow of the real thing.

When the Roman army came through and destroyed the Temple, *it confirmed that the day of embracing shadows was finished and God wanted humanity to embrace the sacrifice of His Son*. The destruction of Jerusalem was not a manifestation of God's anger at the Jews, but it was the revelation of His passion towards them. It was the manifestation of His desire for them to walk in relationship to Him as Father and friend instead of law-giver and judge.

God has no problem shaking up and even destroying our religious systems and structures that we embrace in the place of Him. Those who embraced the Old System were actually embracing it to their own detriment. Many Christians fled the city (because of Jesus warning them in Matthew 24) and were saved. But many, who had not believed Jesus, stayed and defended the

Temple — to their death.

The A.D. 70 destruction of the Jerusalem Temple was the fulfillment of the *shaking* that had been prophesied by the writer of Hebrews. Everything was shaken and the Kingdom of God that had come in Christ remained.

Look at Hebrews 12:26-27:

"At that time his voice shook the earth, but now he has promised, "Once more I will shake not only the earth but also the heavens." The words "once more" indicate the removing of what can be shaken--that is, created things--so that what cannot be shaken may remain." Hebrews 12:26-27 (NIV)

NO MIXTURE

You can't mix grace and law. You can't mix the old system with the new. You can't put old wine in a new wineskin. You can't hold on to *shadows* when the *substance* is standing right in front of you!

The danger of the early Hebrew church was that they continued to embrace grace and law — the old and the new — their works and His work. You cannot go both ways. Paul stated it clearly to the Galatians who wanted to keep working for their salvation and sanctification:

__19__"For through the law I died to the law so that I might live for God. __20__I have been crucified with Christ and I no longer live, but Christ lives in me. The life I now live in the body, I live by faith in the Son of God, who loved me and gave himself for me. __21__I do not set aside the grace of God, for if righteousness could be gained through the law, Christ died for nothing!" Galatians 2:19-21 (NIV)

You don't have to add your part to the mix. Trusting in our own works is like taking the grace of God and putting it in the backseat while you take the wheel of your own spirituality. It's not a good idea ☺

My advice to you is this: go ahead and take the backseat. Hand over the wheel to Jesus and let His grace take you on the journey of being holy and joyful living apart from your own works.

If all of this *quitting-talk* makes you frustrated or angry, that's okay! It made me angry as well. I was a pretty zealous religionist in the past....

Fasting weekly, praying 3+ hours per day, reading my bible pretty religiously and condemning myself if I didn't talk to people about Jesus almost everywhere I went; those are just a few things that describe my life before I was touched by the revelation of grace.

Letting go of religious efforts was like someone stripping drugs from an addict. I soon began to realize that I had been the master of my own spirituality.

You might be in the same boat as I was — trusting in your spiritual disciplines and efforts to keep you strong in the faith. Here are some good questions to ask yourself:

1. On the days that you don't get to spend time in focused prayer and bible reading, do you feel *further from God* or *less spiritual* than on days that you do those things?
2. If you stumble in any kind of sin, do you feel *less spiritual* or like you can't approach God confidently and with joy?
3. Do you always feel like you could be and should be *doing more* for God?
4. Do you live with a sense that God is disappointed in you?
5. Do you live with a sense of peace, joy, and contentment regardless of your performance?

If you answered *yes* to any of these questions (1-4) and *no* to question 5, then I have good news for you! You are up for retirement. That's right. Retire. Rest. Take a good ole' nap in the glorious gospel. Retire and live on full-Kingdom benefits.

Jesus did the job that you couldn't do, and He is faithful to keep you. You didn't save yourself, and you can't keep yourself saved. You are a Son and not a slave. You don't owe God *anything;* **absolutely nothing.** You never did. He was never banking on you to make up for your failures and faults. He took care of those long before you ever realized it.

You are *perfectly clean, perfectly loved,* and *perfectly forgiven.* Today, retire from your works and enter into the *rest* of the gospel.

CHAPTER 2
THE BATTLE IS OVER
No Longer Sinners, But Saints!

Back in December of 2011 a group of *zealous revivalists* and I gathered to cry out to God in repentance and bring a *shift* to the *spiritual atmosphere* of our city. We all came together in order to pray and bring about *revival* in our city.

We believed God had ordained us all to be the truth-bearers in our city. Of course, that was true, but we were a little bit confused about the exclusivity of such a claim. The end of the extreme religious mindset is always **exclusivity** — believing that *we* are the answer to *their* problem.

That's definitely what we believed.

We were chosen by God to help all of the *others* who weren't willing or able to *pay the price* to see the city changed. Some of this might sound like a foreign language to most of you, and honestly, I hope it does.

But to others, you know exactly what I'm talking about — it's religious exclusivity at its finest — and it's psychotic at its core.

At first, the gatherings were very powerful and encouraging. We had wonderful times of worship and enjoyable times *soaking* in the tangible presence of Holy Spirit. But the more we met, the more we began trying to *sense God's direction* based upon our subjective experiences — be it dreams, visions, or impressions we sensed.

Many felt we needed to *get ourselves cleaned up* in order to *go deeper* with God.

At one point we had a *prophet* from the city come to our meeting and pray over each of us individually. He spent time praying *bad spirits* off of us. Unfortunately, some of the words he spoke were more discouraging than encouraging for people in our group.

This is the interesting thing about folks who *work in the prophetic gifting.* If they don't have the *goodness of God* and the *work of Christ on the cross* as their filter for all they *see and sense,* then they can actually do more harm than good. Even if what they *see* is from God, their interpretation can get really awkward.[1]

Been there, done that, bought the T-Shirt.

And of course, I burned that shirt

once I heard the **gospel**.

Eventually our meetings became like *self-cleansing, repentance* sessions in which we were instructed by whoever may have heard from God that week to *search ourselves for sin* and then repent of that sin during the hour and a half meetings.

Talk about *depressing*.

That's the problem with religion. It always leaves you lacking. It

---

[1] Many who have the gift of prophecy often find themselves living solely from their dreams and visions and only interpreting Scripture based off of their own *prophetic experiences*. This is very dangerous for individuals but can be catastrophic when that individual begins leading others based off of the same premises. The prophetic is a powerful gift to be used in abundance by the Body of Christ, but it must be used in context to the finished work of Christ or it will quickly become counterproductive for a spiritual community. Simply put, *always interpret dreams, visions and prophetic utterances* through the filter of what Christ has already accomplished on the cross according to the New Testament revelation.

always tells you there is more work to be done. It always demands something and doesn't lift a finger to help you out. It is the never-ending hamster wheel that keeps you running after the dangling carrot you will never catch.

Well, not until you **die,** of course.

And what is that dangling carrot that religion promises?

What is the ultimate goal of our religious efforts?

Holiness. Righteousness. Goodness.

And ultimately… *Perfection.*

If you've spent more than a couple Sunday's in Church, then you have probably heard something like this,

"None of us are perfect. We are all on the journey."

"Only God is holy. We are still just sinners saved by grace."

"Someday, when we die, we will be perfect in the sweet by and by."

"Well, don't get too cocky, young man. You'll never be perfect or holy until you get to heaven."

Really? **Death** is my guarantee of holiness? **Death** is my sure sanctification?

So you are telling me that I have been "*saved*" into a religious system that keeps me feeling bad for every bad thing I do, but I am *destined* to continue doing those *bad things* until **I die?**

That's rather unfortunate news, and it's definitely not a club I'd want to join.

What have we been saved *from* and what have we been saved *into*?

Most Christians will tell you we've been saved from *hell* and saved *into heaven*.

But could it be **bigger** than that? And possibly **better** than that?

TODAY, YOU HAVE ARRIVED

Folks are tired of seeing pictures of the damned and hearing ideas of a mystical heaven that seems to have almost nothing in common with concrete reality. And the message of hell has done more to push people away from God than it has to bring them to Him.

People have concluded they'd rather go to hell with their friends than hang out in heaven with a God who sends people to hell. I don't blame them.

I do believe in a literal heaven, and I do believe in a literal hell. But I do not and will not espouse to a definition of the gospel that has more to do with heaven and hell than it does with the Person and work of Jesus Christ on the cross.

We haven't only been saved from a future hell, but we've been saved from a present hell. The state of living in constant deception about the character and nature of God, believing that He is the god who is against us, is a *living hell itself*.

Adam's fallen mind and the fallen nature passed on through his fruit binge was the initial taste of a present hell that we all inherited. But Christ and His sabotage of our sinful existence was the solution that brought us to the *now reality* of our heavenly experience.

We *have been* seated with Christ in heavenly places (Ephesians 2:6).

We *have been* made partakers of the divine nature (2 Peter 1:4).

We *have been* hidden in Christ and absorbed completely in God (Colossians 3:1-3).

As much as we talk about the *future,* we often miss the truth about the *present.*

The divine message is less about a *future hope* and more about a *present reality* that only gets better and better and goes from *glory to glory.* Don't get me wrong. Yes, it is about the future. But it is just as much about *now.*

All we have is now — the present.

That's why the writer says, *"Today is the day of salvation." (2 Corinthians 6:2)*

It's pointless to get hung up on *the future* because all that we truly have within our grasp is *today – right now.*

We are only going from *glory to glory, from now to now.* And thankfully, Christ is within us *now,* and He is the *now expectation* of our today-glory and our future-glory (Colossians 1:27).

The Apostle Paul and the other boys never relegated God's good news to a future possibility that we would get *if we do our best* to be good Christians. Instead, the message was a declaration of something that God did on our behalf that we get to take part in through our simple recognition that we all have been included in His love.

Our future is something we partake in by partaking in *today.* Many relegate *heaven, perfection,* and freedom from the *sinful nature* to a day far away; something that we will eventually attain to when we *die.*

But, if **death** is our freedom from *imperfection,* then go ahead and consider yourself **dead.**

This is what Paul said. Check it out:

*"Even so consider yourselves to be **dead to sin**, but alive to God in Christ Jesus." Romans 6:11 (NASB)*

*"For **you have died** and your life is hidden with Christ in God." Colossians 3:3 (NASB)*

The declaration of our salvation is about what has **been done** through the work of Christ. He became our *sinful self*, our *imperfect self*, and we became *His perfection.*

"He made Him who knew no sin to be sin on our behalf, so that we might become the righteousness of God in Him." 2 Corinthians 5:21 (NASB)

When He died on the cross, our imperfect self died along with Him.

All of our failures died. All of our mistakes were crucified.

All of our negative emotions were buried. [2]

Once...and...for...all.

Perfection has been paid for.

*"For by one offering He has **perfected** for all time those who are sanctified." Hebrews 10:14 (NASB)*

You

are

perfect.

---

[2] This is not a promise that you'll never *feel* a *negative emotion* but the declaration that you are free from its power and it is not the true you. Simply count yourself dead to sin and its negativity and alive to God in Christ Jesus (Romans 6:11). At first you may have to do this quite a bit, but as we sink deep into this truth we begin to find that our lives manifest this reality without trying.

Completeness has been given freely.

*"For in Him all the fullness of Deity dwells in bodily form, and **in Him** you have been made **complete**," Colossians 2:9-10 (NASB)*

You

are

complete.

God had to deal with *sin*. And the root of sin was the knowledge of good and evil: the false reality that there is *another way* to live in perfection outside of friendship with Him.

It is the deception of *self-effort* and the lie that says *humanity has defects*. It is the lie that man wasn't made perfect and that we were *not good*. But God made man and declared, "It is **good**." Somewhere along the way, we stopped believing that and started trying to *become good*. Sure, sin tainted us. But before sin had tainted us, Jesus sainted us.

*"He chose us in Him before the foundation of the world, that we would be **holy** and **blameless** before Him" Ephesians 1:4 (NASB)*

Sin could never steal our origin, and it could never change our design.

Mankind's problem was in our head. We believed the lie that we lacked something, so we gave into the deception to try and gain something. When we did this, we entered a lower domain of unbelief and our understanding was darkened by deception.

Our eyes became *evil* and *darkened,* and the world we began to see, we saw through a darkened lens of unbelief.

Unbelief in what?

In *God's goodness*

In *our origin*

In our *eternal identity as His children*

We began seeing our *Father as a Judge* and our *Friend as a Foe*. God saw fit to come and deal with this darkened understanding, this Adam-ic idea.

So He came, in the form of weakened and frail mankind, susceptible to our sin and struggle, yet walking in complete victory over our darkened mindsets. He came and became our brokenness in order to completely destroy it once and for all.

FOR US, AS US, TOWARDS US

He didn't leave us to our own devices and our own solutions. Instead, He made the decision *for us* and took care of the problem *as us*. In doing this, He showed us His continued and unbreakable commitment *toward us*.

While we were still His enemies, Christ died for us (see Romans 5:8).

He laid down His life for those who didn't want anything to do with Him because He knew that we had forgotten who we were. We had given in to the false identity.

That old Adam-ic self was full of deceit and destined to die:

Not as a punishment *for sin*

but as the result *of sin.*

Christ came to reveal the Father, not to appease the Father. Christ came to express God's love for us. He came to show us God's love, not to make God love us. God never stopped loving us. He has always and will always love humanity.

He decided, apart from a conference call with us, to take on the death that we inherited as a result of sin. He did not desire to continue His existence without us. He made us for Himself and planned an eternal friendship with us. He wouldn't have it any other way. So what did He do? He died *for us* and He died *as us.*

He tasted death and separation on behalf of us all.

*"But we do see Him who was made for a little while lower than the angels, namely, Jesus, because of the suffering of death crowned with glory and honor, so that by the grace of God He might **tasted death for everyone.**" Hebrews 2:9 (NASB)*

Not that God needed a sacrifice, but we did. The cross didn't change God's mind about us. Rather it changed our minds about God. Jesus showed us that God was not angry with humanity, but humanity had become angry with God.

Not only did He show us what God was like, but in His death, He mystically swallowed up our fallen nature and the separate sinful self that man had created through unbelief and He rendered it powerless.

Not only did He die *for us,* but He died *as us.* Just as Adam sinned *as us (Romans 5:15-17),* Christ did the same and decided to die *as us (Romans 5:18).*

In His death He became *us* and destroyed the *individual, separate, fallen identity* that we had created in Adam. He became the false identity that we had taken on and completely obliterated it in His death on the cross.

That is why Paul emphatically says, *"When One died **all died,**" in 2 Corinthians 5:14.*

Today, I can emphatically declare that you are no longer a sinner.

You no longer have a *sinful nature*.

You are perfect.

You are holy.

You are complete.

You are *good*.

And it's *not your fault*.

Christ has swallowed you up in His life and death. Your life is now hidden with Christ inside of the Ocean of God's love for all humanity. This is *who you are*.

Jesus Christ's work was effective for you.

"Well, why do I still feel imperfect?"

Probably because you have yet to hear this good news.

It's time to awaken to reality. Calculate the cross.

See that you were in Him when He died.

And consider yourself as dead to sin as

Abraham Lincoln is to this world.

Dead, gone, kapeesh.

I love the way the Knox translation says it:

"We have died, once for all, to sin; can we breathe its air again?"
Romans 6:2 (Knox Translation)

You have been included in Christ's effective, completed work on the cross. You have been translated out of darkness, unbelief, depression, sickness, and sadness. All the affects of sin and the curse are no longer yours to embrace. That world is gone. *Can you breathe its air again?* You are free to breathe the air of heaven. You are free to enjoy your ever-lasting life today (John 17:3).

When Jesus said, *"It is finished,"* He was not making a half-hearted declaration regarding His work on the cross. No. His plan was all-inclusive and His work was fully finished. He left no part of your being out of the equation of His death and resurrection. You are not a perfect *spirit*, with an imperfect *soul* and a jacked up body.

Sure, our experience tells us differently at times, but we don't live by our experience, we live by the faith of the Son of God. You weren't partially *crucified with Christ*. You were fully included in His crucifixion. Your only job is to recognize this reality and set your mind on that truth.

I have been crucified with Christ. I no longer live but Christ lives in me and the life I now live, I live by the faith of the Son of God who loved me and gave Himself for me. (see Galatians 2:20)

Paul got it. He understood that Christ's death was a vicarious one on our behalf, and our efforts to include ourselves were not needed. Paul realized that within the body of Jesus was the entire human race and every bit of the false reality we had created through our rebellion.

Look what Paul said regarding our inclusion in Christ's death...

He says that when one died, all died. (2 Corinthians 5:14) Who was that one? Christ, of course. And who are the *all?* Everyone, of course.

God didn't wait for you to be born in order to take care of your fallen nature. He didn't wait for you to *get right with Him* before He chose to forgive you in Christ.

Paul said in Romans 5 that *while we were still helpless,* Christ died for the ungodly. And that Jesus demonstrates His undying love towards us by dying for us when we didn't want anything to do with Him (see Romans 5:6-8).

Could it be that while we were still unable to do *anything* for ourselves, He did *everything* for us and *as us?*

What if He did what we could not do for ourselves, without our request or permission?

It seems a little unfair. We want to do *our part.* But He didn't wait for us to have any part. He went for the whole enchilada and then some…

Look what Paul had to say about humanity's failure to do *our part:*

"Therefore, just as through one man sin entered into the world, and death through sin, and so death spread to all men, because all sinned." *Romans 5:12 (NASB)*

And just who did He do this for? For the ones who lived right, prayed right, read enough King James Bible, took enough non-alcoholic communions and never smoked a cigarette?

Or was it for the ones whom He arbitrarily chose? You know, *the select few who made the cut out of His sovereign-all-powerful-beyond-comprehension-divine-selection?*

Hmmmmm...???

Could it be that **no one** could make the cut? Could it be that Christ's work was as effective as Adam's toward all humanity? Could it be that it was *even more effective?*

As unfair as the sinful effect that came upon us *all,* so it is with the heavenly effect.

Yet, Paul seems to say that it was similar but not the same. In fact, he declares that the effect of Christ's work on the cross for *all* humanity was *"much more"* effective and far outweighed Adam's failure.

Check it out →

*"But the free gift is not like the transgression. For if by the transgression of the one <u>the many died</u>, **much more did the grace of God** and the gift by the grace of the one Man, Jesus Christ, <u>abound to the many</u>." Romans 5:15 (NASB)*

Through Adam's sin *many* died. Through Christ's death and resurrection, the *many* were influenced by grace.

Paul goes on to say in verse 16 that the gift *is not like the trespass.* The sin of Adam condemned all. But the gift is *much better!* The gift of grace was given to all resulting in justification!

The judgment of *guilt* was passed on everyone because of what Adam did. But in contrast, the free gift came to humanity declaring *justification* and *right-standing* before God.

Adam's fall was **swallowed up** by Jesus' final act on the cross.

So, what is there to do?

Well, passively receive and rest in what He has done and watch the fruit of *"reigning in life"* begin manifesting in your circumstances and your living. Paul says in verse 17 of Romans 5 that those who *receive the gift* of grace will reign in life through that gift.

"Receiving the gift" doesn't make the gift yours. The gift was yours before you ever believed it. Receiving the gift means that you actually begin experiencing in reality the truth of what has already been given. Basically, start enjoying it!

Paul finishes up this section by nailing the coffin shut with an all-inclusive declaration of God's righteousness revealed through Christ:

"So then as through <u>one transgression there resulted condemnation to all men</u>, even so through <u>one act of righteousness there resulted justification of life to all men</u>. 19 For as through the one man's disobedience <u>the many were made sinners</u>, even so through the obedience of the One <u>the many will be made righteous</u>." Romans 5:18-19 (NASB)

Jesus finished the job on the tree. In His one act He declared that you have been made righteous in Him.

What Adam did, Jesus undid.

What Adam tainted, Jesus sainted.

He became our sin and we became His rightness.

He became our darkness and we became His light.

He became our failure and we became His success.

Your identity is completely found in Him and as Him. You don't get your own separate cross; you were united with Him on His cross. You were baptized into His death and raised to newness of life.

*3 Or do you not know that all of us who have been baptized into Christ Jesus have been **baptized into His death**? 4 Therefore we have been buried with Him through baptism into death, so that as Christ was raised from the dead through the glory of the Father, so we too might walk in newness of life. Romans 6:3-4 (NASB)*

Paul is not talking about your personal baptismal in Pastor Jim's swimming pool. I mean, sure, he is speaking in part of what you did when you were dunked or sprinkled in the holy chlorine water in your Pastor's backyard or the muddy-holy water at your churches *lake day*. But that was really only a representation of what took place 2,000 years ago when Christ baptized humanity into His death.

Your **baptism** didn't save you.

Your **confession** didn't save you.

Your **prayer** didn't save you.

Christ saved you.

When He died, you died. When He was raised, you were raised. He only gets one death and you only get one death. *In the same way* that He died once to sin, you did too.

His death was yours and that's a fact. He died *for us* and *as us*. He didn't wait for our permission to die our death, and He didn't wait for our consent to include us in His life. He chose and He acted.

"For the death that He died, He died to sin once for all; but the life that He lives, He lives to God. 11 Even so consider yourselves to be dead to sin, but alive to God in Christ Jesus." Romans 6:10-11

Your sinful nature was completely taken care of 2,000 years ago when Christ died.

"...and in Him you were also circumcised with a circumcision made without hands, in the removal of the body of the flesh by the circumcision of Christ." Colossians 2:11 (NASB)

*"In union with Christ you were circumcised, not with the circumcision that is made by human beings, but with the circumcision made by Christ, which consists of **being freed from the power of this sinful self**." Colossians 2:11 (Good News Translation)*

Just as circumcision could not be done by the child himself, but had to be done by another, so Christ is the one who has circumcised our hearts and removed the dirty old sinful nature without any assistance from us. This is great news!

You are no longer a sinner. You were included in the death, burial, and resurrection of Christ through His faithfulness. His pain was your gain. His death was your death, and His life is now your life.

Think about your worst failure,

your greatest regret,

your haunting memories...

Each and every one of those

were dealt with on the cross of Christ,

and they no longer define you AT ALL.

Those mistakes are no longer *your mistakes*. They were actions done by a person who had *forgotten* their original design but who has now been awakened to the truth of their inclusion in grace.

Today, count yourself as being completely *dead* to the old you. Have a little funeral for it if needs be, but don't live another day in relation to it.

Count yourself as being one who was dead and is now alive, wakened from the deathly sleep of unbelief. See yourself as perfect, holy, and beautiful. Look in the mirror and see the beauty of God shining right back at you.

You are loved. You are holy. You are perfect. You are accepted.

CHAPTER 3
WITCHCRAFT, HARRY POTTER,
AND THE GOD WHO VOTES REPUBLICAN
What the Gospel is NOT

We all have preconceived ideas of who God is and how He acts towards people. We all expect Him to fit into our ideological, philosophical, and theological constructs that we grew up with or have embraced as mature adults.

I mean, if He doesn't fit those things, then we might actually have to *change* what we think. *God forbid!* Most of our ideas about God and how He relates with people are based on how and where we grow   up.

For me, I was a southern grown boy. And growing up in Texas during the *Bush-Dynasty,* you would think that being right-wing is almost equal to being born-again. If you've ever lived in the South, then you know what I'm talking about. If not, then you might be better for it.

THE DAY THE WEST LOST OUR WAY

If you've grown up in the United States or in the West, then you've probably heard *the gospel* more times than you care to remember; well, at least some version of it.

It seems that somewhere during this journey of church history, we veered way off course. Strangely enough, Jesus isn't at the helm of the ship, but instead at the back taking a nice nap. During all of the storms of heretical non-sense, Jesus will wake up and give a playful smirk toward His kids and then turn to remind the waves-of-confusion who is actually in charge.

Even though we've taken a ton of detours, He keeps us in the same ocean and always gets us back on course; often using messy revivals, temperamental-reformers, and *famous TV preachers*.

One massive detour that the church has taken has to do with our expression and definition of the *gospel*. Somehow it's become more of an *invitation* rather than the great *declaration* that it's meant to be.

This is not anything new. Ever since the Apostle Paul himself began declaring the message that Jesus gave him, the church has been bending and distorting it to fit its own comforts.

Don't think that by using the word *"comfort,"* I am only talking about people who seem to make the gospel sound too simple and easy. Comfort has less to do with making something *easy* and more to do with making it fit within our current belief system. It's much more *comfortable* to stick with what we've always heard than it is to go through the uncomfortable process of *changing our minds*.

I'm actually talking about those who like to make the gospel sound like you can't get in except *by the skin of your own teeth*; those who would say you can't get in without *pumping up your own faith, and you can't stay in unless you hold tightly to the reigns of the wild rodeo bull they call **faith***. If this version of the *gospel* sounds all too familiar to you, then read on because you're about to get set free.

HARRY POTTER AND SECRET WITCHES

Spending the last nine years in the *Charismatic* brand of the church, I have heard some of the craziest ideas that I don't have the time or the energy to talk about here. But there is one word that would get thrown around quite a bit and I will mention it here: *witchcraft*.

When we hear of witchcraft, many of us imagine ghosts and goblins following behind a woman on a broomstick coming to turn you into a frog. Of course, we all know that those things are fairy tales. But we also know that witchcraft and the occult is very real, and it's definitely a false form of spirituality.

When the church talks about witchcraft, it comes in all kinds of fearful-conspiratorial packages.

"Don't let your kids watch Harry Potter or they'll become...witches,"

or

"Don't talk to Satanists or you might get deceived."

Frankly, both of these ideas are plain silly.

Did you know that the only time the idea of *witchcraft* is

mentioned in the New Testament is in the book of Galatians?

Look what Paul wrote to them in Galatians 3:1 —

You foolish Galatians, who has bewitched you, before whose eyes Jesus Christ was publicly portrayed as crucified? (NASB Translation)

You stupid Galatians! Who has put you under a spell? Before your very eyes, Yeshua the Messiah was clearly portrayed as having been put to death as a criminal! (CJB Translation)

You stupid Galatians! I told you exactly how Jesus Christ was nailed to a cross. Has someone now put an evil spell on you? (CEV Translation)

Paul calls out the Galatian church and accuses them of falling prey to blatant witchcraft. No, they didn't watch Harry Potter movies or get invaded by secret witches who cast spells on their church services. (I've heard both of these ideas in the Charismatic church).

So, what was the spell they fell under?

Simply put: they stopped believing the gospel.

They were convinced to change the real definition of grace, which they had just recently believed, to something that fit comfortably into their old religious belief system.

The Galatians had recently come out of the old system of the Law of Moses. They had worked very hard to keep the commandments and accomplish righteousness through their works. When Paul came to town declaring the gospel to them, they received the message gladly and gave up their works-based striving. They saw powerful miracles among them as they simply trusted in Christ's reconciling work on the cross that provided everything for them.

Massive kudos to these guys. Seriously. They laid it all down.

Well, at least for a few weeks.

COLLECTING TIPS

After Paul passed through Galatia, some old friends of his decided to stop in town and encourage the brethren with some *follow-up ministry* to the Galatian church. These guys were called *Judiazers (AKA the Circumcision Party)*. They were notorious for following Paul in order to persecute him.

Often, these guys would preach in the churches that Paul just finished ministering to and throw them into a ton of confusion. What was the confusion? Well, they weren't telling them to go back and follow the entire Law of Moses.

No, it was much more subtle than that.

There was an old custom in the Jewish belief called *circumcision*. God gave this practice to Abraham as a sign of the covenant between God and the descendants of Abraham.

10 This is My covenant, which you shall keep, between Me and you and your descendants after you: every male among you shall be circumcised. 11 And you shall be circumcised in the flesh of your foreskin, and it shall be the sign of the covenant between Me and you. Genesis 17:10-11 (NASB)

We're all adults here, I assume, so I think we know what this means. If not, ask your Dad (and take a picture of his facial reaction). This was a painful process, and it was done when the child was eight days old. It was something that had to be *done to* the child since he was unable to do it for himself.

All of this was pointing to a greater reality.

"and in Him you were also circumcised with a circumcision made without hands, in the <u>removal of the body of the flesh</u> by the <u>circumcision of Christ</u>." Colossians 2:11 (NASB)

Back to the main point. The Judaizers.

These guys were like bad waiters. They showed up, took the order, fed you leftovers from yesterday, and then demanded a tip…literally.

Paul called them the *circumcision party*. They prided themselves in adding the requirement of circumcision to the simple gospel message. It's even said that they wore belts that had a place to hang the *tips* that they had received at their meetings.

Like a bad televangelists counting offerings, these guys boasted in how many circumcisions they performed.

Imagine this semi-sermon from the circumcision guys:

"We are so glad that you have all received the gospel! Paul is a wonderful preacher, and we are so honored to follow up and build on the foundation that he laid last week at the conference. We really do appreciate Paul, but his teaching only touches the surface of true Christianity and spirituality. Now, do you guys want to be radical for Christ? Do you want to know the deep things of God? Are you hungry for more of God? We have the answer for you… step right up and receive the circumcision that was commanded by our forefather Abraham. This is guaranteed to take you to the next level in your walk with God."

And…the Galatians fell for it.

The dudes, from young to old, all made the cut.

PAUL TAGGED THE GALATIANS IN A LONG FACEBOOK POST

Paul heard about the mess that was taking place in Galatia and decided to write a *Facebook* status and tag these kiddos from Galatia:

6 I am astonished that you are so quickly deserting the one who called you to live in the grace of Christ and are turning to a different gospel — 7 which is really no gospel at all. Evidently some people are throwing you into confusion and are trying to pervert the gospel of Christ. 8 But even if we or an angel from heaven should preach a gospel other than the one we preached to you, let them be under God's curse! 9 As we have already said, so now I say again: If anybody is preaching to you a gospel other than what you accepted, let them be under God's curse!" Galatians 1:6-9 (NIV)

Wow. You'd think that there was some massive deception going on at the Galatian church. Maybe some form of gospel that allowed people to sleep around, conduct homosexual marriages, and watch R-rated movies. Nope. Just circumcision.

He goes as far as to say that if anyone is adding anything to the gospel, then that person should be accursed.

"Come on, Paul. Do you really have to go that far? It's just a little snip. And it was in the Old Covenant. Can't we just add a little bit of our own actions and efforts into this thing?"

Absolutely not.

Look what he says about their distortion of the gospel:

Oh, foolish Galatians! Who has cast an <u>evil spell</u> on you? For the meaning of Jesus Christ's death was made as clear to you as if you had seen a picture of his death on the cross. 2 Let me ask you this one

*question: Did you receive the Holy Spirit by obeying the law of Moses?
Of course not! You received the Spirit because you believed the message
you heard about Christ. 3 How foolish can you be? After starting your
Christian lives in the Spirit, why are you now trying to become perfect
by your own human effort?" Galatians 3:1-3 (NIV)*

Again, this is all about the *little add-on* of circumcision. Look what
Paul says here about those who actually go through with the snip:

*2 Mark my words! I, Paul, tell you that if you let yourselves be
circumcised, Christ will be of no value to you at all. 3 Again I declare to
every man who lets himself be circumcised that he is obligated to obey the
whole law. 4 You who are trying to be justified by the law have been
alienated from Christ; you have fallen away from grace. (Galatians 5:2-4
NIV)*

I can see it now. The folks in Galatia responding on the Facebook
thread:

*"No value? Smh... Wait a second, Paul. You're saying that if we go
through with this little add-on for spiritual advancement, then Christ
has become of no value to us? I thought that Christ was the foundation
and now I need to add my works to the equation? I mean, the reason I'm
getting circumcised is because I'm responding to God's love for me. I'm
showing the Lord how dedicated I am to Him. I am giving Him my all
(literally). And, of course, I'm using His grace to help me go through
with this. No value? That seems a little overboard, Paul. You need to
balance out grace with works, brother."*

This sounds absurd to us, nowadays. We would never fall for this!
This is obvious spiritual manipulation and a clear add-on to the
gospel. Well, it wasn't so clear to them and hindsight always
seems to be 20/20. Every time-period and culture has its legalistic
vices. Circumcision just so happened to be the deception of their
time.

The circumcision deception takes on many different forms throughout history. But every time it rears its ugly head, it's always marked by this same fruit in the lives of the people who subscribed to it: *frustration, depression, and self-destruction.*

So what spiritual *add-ons* have we so easily accepted that have taken our eyes off of the simplicity of the gospel?

THE "GOOD NEWS" OF SELF-DENIAL

I remember speaking on the phone recently with my friend, Jacob. He shared deep internal conflicts with me regarding his desire to work hard, make a lot of money, and take care of his family, and how he felt this was in opposition to everything he had learned about seeking first *the kingdom.* I could hear the turmoil in his voice, and I had heard it before. He currently works at an A/C company and recently received a promotion—which he was soberly excited about.

"Blaise, sometimes I wonder if my desire to have a good job and make good money is getting in the way of seeking God's kingdom. Maybe I should just move to Africa and do missions work or something," he said.

This wasn't anything new. I had heard this line of thinking *many* times over the years as I've worked constantly with college-aged students and teenagers. Often I find that many young people feel a tension between following their dreams and *doing ministry* or *doing Kingdom work.*

The truth is that a small minority (around 2%) are actually called to vocational ministry. The other 98% of human beings will probably never (and should never) get paid to stand in a pulpit to preach or sit and counsel/disciple others. Now, that doesn't mean that only 2% of people will actually *minister* to others.

**That's
absurd.**

In fact, there are those who will *never* hold a microphone or stand in a pulpit who will actually be *more influential* in the body of Christ than preachers and teachers. It really doesn't matter whether you are a part of the 2% or the 98%. Everyone has their gifting and calling, and no one should be sitting around trying to be something they're not. If everyone was in *vocational ministry,* then we'd have a pretty dull world. Imagine, preachers everywhere...

Wait...no. Stop imagining that. Seriously, **stop**.

Unfortunately, in the last 20-30 years of Western Christianity we have, with great intentions, created a Christian culture that feels the necessity to give up its dreams in order to follow *God's call*. All of our missions organizations and *ministry schools* have done little to make an actual dent in what we call *the great commission* but have in return pumped out a generation who thinks they have to do *vocational ministry* in order to be spiritual.

I've literally watched young people become a Christian, then go directly into a *ministry school* or start working at a *ministry base* only to find that 5 years later they are still volunteering there with absolutely no desire to do vocational ministry.

Then comes the disillusionment of leaving the ministry school and finding out that colleges don't care at all about what you learned there, and real jobs don't acknowledge what you did at the *missions school* as being legitimate work (and often for good reason).[3]

Some of these young people recover, move on, and work hard to become an effective part of society. Some remain confused and caught up in a western subculture of trying to live off of missions support for the next 20 years. Those are the extreme cases, but if you've been a pastor or youth pastor for more than a week, then you know exactly what I am talking about.

Back to my story about Jacob…

So I asked him, *"Jacob, what makes you think that working a good job and supporting your family is in opposition to seeking first the Kingdom? What if the Kingdom is actually within you like Jesus said it was? What if kingdom work is actually just being who God created you to be and enjoying your life in the process?"*

This was a brain twister for my buddy, Jacob. *"You don't think that's selfish?"* he asked.

"No freakin way, dude," I said emphatically. *"You no longer live, but Christ lives in you. And He put His desires within you and created you to do things that only you can do. He doesn't want you to try to be something different than what He created you to be."*

"Hmmm…" I could hear at the other end of the line.

I continued with my pseudo-sermon…

"When you start seeing yourself according to the gospel, then you start seeing that old selfish-self as dead, and you begin seeing the New Man alive in Christ Jesus. You suddenly realize that you are free to LIVE your life according to the New Creation; you are free to live life abundantly, free from fear and with great boldness regarding the future. I'm going for

---

[3] I am **not** talking about legitimate theological seminary. I am speaking mostly about non-accredited *ministry schools and long-term ministry internships*. I would highly recommend doing an accredited seminary or bible college for ministry training or *short term* internships that don't take all of your college years and all of your money.

my dreams, and I'm going to do them for Jesus and with Jesus! You should too, bro!"

"Hmmm... I'll have to think about that, man," he said.

Well, at least he's open to *thinking.*

What is it about Christianity that makes people think they have to sacrifice their dreams and goals for the sake of *the Kingdom?* If you are trying to sacrifice your dreams on the altar of God's calling then I'd encourage you to stop and actually talk to God about those dreams.

You might be surprised to find out that many of those dreams are things He placed in you and have more to do with "God's calling" on your life than doing some kind of "ministry work" that you actually don't want to do. Everyone has his or her place. Don't try to fill someone else's shoes just because they look more *spiritual* than yours.

WHAT ABOUT DYING TO SELF?

This is the question that always comes up when I start talking about this topic.

"But, Blaise, Jesus said that we need to deny ourselves, take up our cross, and follow Him?"

Context is key when interpreting Scripture. Everything Jesus spoke, He spoke to real people at a real time in history. We simply cannot make the mistake of taking everything that Jesus said and applying it directly to our lives.

We must understand His point and the principle of what He was speaking and interpret it through the lens of the finished work of the Cross.

Context: In His life on earth, Jesus spoke to the Jewish people *before* He went to the cross. When Jesus spoke to the Jews about *denying themselves,* it was clear that none of them had received the revelation of their crucifixion with Christ and their co-resurrection with him — because that revelation had not yet been released.

Jesus *often* spoke in parables and in stories with no intention of fully explaining Himself. Even the guys closest to Him, the twelve, often didn't understand the point of Jesus' parables and sayings.

Of course, after His resurrection things started to become very clear. Even still, it wasn't until good ole' Apostle Paul came along that things actually became crystal clear, and we began to understand the implications of Christ's death for those who believe and also for the entire world.

In the same way that we must interpret the Old Testament through the lens of Christ, we must interpret Christ's pre-cross words through the lens of the New Covenant revelation given *by Jesus Christ to the Apostle Paul.*

With that in mind, we cannot imagine that we should take Jesus' words in the gospels and try to interpret them with any coherent understanding apart from the words of Paul in the epistles. What words of Paul am I speaking of? Let me take a moment and toss a few important points of Paul out on the table:

"6 For we know that <u>our old self was crucified with him</u> so that the body ruled by sin might be done away with, that we should no longer be slaves to sin — 7 because anyone who has died has been set free from sin. 8 Now if we died with Christ, we believe that we will also live with him. 9 For

we know that since Christ was raised from the dead, he cannot die again; death no longer has mastery over him. 10 The death he died, <u>he died to sin once for all</u>; but the life he lives, he lives to God. 11 <u>In the same way</u>, count yourselves <u>dead to sin</u> but <u>alive to God</u> in Christ Jesus." Romans 6:6-11 (NIV)

Paul gives a radical declaration regarding the current state of our *old sinful selves*. **Dead.**

That's right, **d-e-a-d.**

There seems to be an understanding from Paul's perspective, that we are not in the business of **dying daily** but rather **recognizing** our *once and for all* death with Christ. Look at verse ten and eleven; Paul declares that Christ died to sin *one time* and "in the same way" we are to understand that His death was our death; and that **death** only happened **one time.**

Check out what He has to say to the Colossians:

"11 In him you were also circumcised with a circumcision not performed by human hands. Your whole self ruled by the flesh was put off when you were circumcised by Christ, 12 having been buried with him in baptism, in which you were also raised with him through your faith in the working of God, who raised him from the dead." Colossians 2:11-12 (NIV)

Paul declares here that our old-life that was ruled by the desire to rebel against God's will has been completely severed from us and that we now live a life that is filled with God's power. We are no longer an *independent agent* trying to figure out life on our own. We have been spiritually swallowed up by the life of Jesus and our life is His life and His life is our life.

"For you have died and your life is hidden with Christ in God."

Colossians 3:3 (NASB)

"I have been crucified with Christ; I no longer live but Christ lives in me, and the life that I live I live by the faith of the Son of God, who loved me and gave himself for me." Galatians 2:20 (see Jubilee 2000 version)

It seems that Holy Spirit is trying to get something across to people all over the world: that they *have died* and *have been raised to new life with Christ*. This puts everything that Jesus said in a new light. Let's go back and look at it again:

"If anyone would come after me, let him deny himself and take up his cross and follow me. 25 For whoever would save his life will lose it, but whoever loses his life for my sake will find it." Matthew 16:24-25 (ESV)

Jesus speaking to these folks about taking up their *cross* would be as awkward as Him speaking to us about carrying around an electric chair. All they knew of the cross was that it was an instrument of death, and they had no clue that it would be the tool through which Jesus would save the world.

Their only view of Jesus was that of a great Prophet or Teacher. Other than that, if any of them did believe He was the Messiah, they mostly expected Him to crucify the Romans not be crucified by them. Jesus dives in and tells them, in essence,

"Guys, if you wanna follow Me, then you're going to have to die. That's what I'm about to do...I'm going to my death. Anyone wanna follow Me to the death instrument? Come on, boys! A good ole' martyrdom!"

I can only imagine the confusion in the camp after such a statement. Jesus had just finished rebuking Peter for being Satanic (right after He had praised him for his great Messianic revelation—see Matthew 16:23). And before that, Jesus told them straight up that he was going to die and rise from the dead (of course, Peter had only heard him say that He would die).

Jesus then goes on to tell them, in essence, that he was going to get strung up on a Roman instrument of torture and be crucified...and, if they wanted to continue to follow the great Messiah, miracle-worker, then they would have to get ready to do the same. I'm sure the disciples were rather confused by all of this.

We know that close to ten of the twelve disciples ended up being crucified for their faith later on. But, before their literal crucifixion, they all experienced a co-crucifixion with Christ at Calvary. Many people die for what they believe, but not everyone realizes *that they have already been crucified with Christ*.

It is clear that Jesus knew something about Himself and about His listeners that no one else knew. The implications of His death would spread far and wide across the face of the earth regardless of whether those living at the time heard about it or knew about it.

His work on the cross was the substitutionary act for all mankind. Just as Adam's sinful act was the effective destroyer of our innocence, so Christ's death was the more-effective restorer of our innocence.

But we cannot partake in Christ's life unless we also effectively partake in His death. Many have taken this idea and twisted it to mean that unless we take up a martyr complex, then we'll never partake in Christ's life. This is popularly called *"The Crucified Life"* in Charismatic circles.

That is not at all what Christ is communicating here.

Sure, some will die for what they believe; but that is not going to happen to the majority of believers. Whether you are killed because of your belief in Christ or live a *normal* life with a family in the suburbs, we are all called to carry the revelation of our co-crucifixion with Christ. We already *have died* and Christ has already *tasted death on our behalf.*

Again, if you'll allow me a little license, then I will do my best to put Jesus' words in context to those to whom He was speaking at the time He was speaking them.

"So I know that you guys have been waiting for your Messiah for many generations. And I know that you were expecting me to knock off the Romans, but that's just not gonna happen. I also know that you've been working hard to keep the commandments and the law so that you'll have right standing with God. I want to tell you that the only way to get right standing with God is to die to yourself. Die to all of your religious striving and your own abilities to please God.

I'm going to the cross, but little do you know, that you are going to the cross with me. In fact, all of humanity is going to that cross with me. And until you identify with my death, you won't realize your resurrection life in me. So, come on boys, let's quit with the self-help religious striving and come to the cross. This is the only way to find true life."

PUT DOWN YOUR CROSS AND TAKE UP HIS LIFE

Jesus didn't want us to go find our own cross to carry. You see, we have to ask the important questions: if Jesus was asking us to *follow Him*, then *where was He going?* Once He picked up *His cross* and *went somewhere... where on earth could He have been headed?*

Well, to Calvary, of course–**to die.** And that happened **once, and only once** (see Romans 6:9-10).

When He carried His cross up to Golgotha, we were *in Him*. When

His hands were nailed, our hands were nailed. When He died, we died. When He was raised, we were raised (see Galatians 2:20 and Colossians 3:3). We don't get our *own death*. He did what we couldn't do.

He doesn't need us to replicate it, but only to <u>realize it</u>.

"The death he died, he died to sin once for all; but the life he lives, he lives to God. In the same way, <u>count yourselves dead to sin</u> but alive to God in Christ Jesus." Romans 6:10-11 (NIV)

If someone wants to live a *crucified life,* then I'd challenge them to consider themselves already dead and raised from the grave.

Some have said,

"Don't try to come down from your personal cross. You have to live a life that recognizes our continual crucifixion; constantly dying to self, etc. etc."

The truth is,

Jesus is no longer on the cross.
And neither are you.
He is fully alive and so are you.

Religion always takes the words of God that are meant to bring life, peace, and joy and turns them into demands that bring death, depression, and destruction. I have watched young and old use these words of Jesus as a means to push their agendas— getting believers to lay down their own dreams and join someone else's ministry cause. But I want to encourage you to see this call to *take up your cross* as good news and not a daily drudge.

PAUL'S DAILY DEATH

This is another problem passage that people always bring up when we start talking about enjoying the life God has given you. *"But Blaise, the Bible says that we have to die daily? How do you fit that into your joyful-living, co-crucified life revelation, eh?"*

Remember, folks, context is always key. You can't pull one verse out of the bible and make an anti-gospel theology out of it. Well, I guess you can, but I wouldn't advise it.

Let's look at the actual verse in context. Paul is speaking to the Corinthian church and reminding them that he has gone to hell and back to preach the gospel of Jesus Christ. There were some in Corinth who were trying to convince them that there was no resurrection of the dead. Paul says to them,

*"Why [if there is no resurrection of the dead] are we also in danger every hour? I affirm, brethren, by the boasting in you which I have in Christ Jesus our Lord, **I die daily.**" 1 Corinthians 15:30-31 (NASB)*

Look what he says in the NIV translation.

*"And as for us, why [if there is no resurrection of the dead] do we endanger ourselves every hour? I **face death every day**." 1 Corinthians 15:30-31 (NIV)*

Paul is saying absolutely nothing about dying to *himself* or anything of that sort. He is simply stating a reality that is happening to him daily because of the fact that he is fulfilling his calling to preach the gospel. Paul was literally almost killed every day.

For some strange reason, preachers take this and yell at little kiddo's telling them that they need to *"die daily like the Apostle Paul said to do."* If that's the case, the *how* do we accomplish this task?

Do we throw ourselves in front of oncoming traffic? (Please don't). Do we make a list of every possession that we own and *enjoy,* then go burn them? Do we all go to the mission field and make sure that we come close to death every day? How about (according to the first part of the verse) *every hour?* So do we die *daily* or do we die *hourly?*

Enough. I'll spare you my continual annoyance with preachers' misuse of this passage. I'll leave you with this quote from John Crowder:

"Religion and suicide are the same spirit; they are both trying to get you to kill what God loves – YOU."

Oh, I almost forgot. There is one more passage I should address very quickly because the sincere believer will always bring it up in context to this conversation.

Romans 8:36 is the other time that Paul mentions *"dying daily"* so let's take a moment and look at the context:

35 Who shall separate us from the love of Christ? Shall trouble or hardship or persecution or famine or nakedness or danger or sword? 36 As it is written: "For your sake we face death all day long; we are *considered as sheep to be slaughtered. 37 No, in all these things we are more than conquerors through him who loved us." Romans 8:35-37*

And again, we understand that this passage is also in context to Paul's persecution and his daily dose of near-death experiences; not to be confused with Paul trying to *kill-off* some kind of internal nature that was not dealt with on the cross of Christ.

More than any, Paul was convinced of his co-crucifixion (Galatians 2:20, Colossians 2:11-12), and he definitely was not bringing a dual message to the Churches of Rome and Corinth –

so let's not read into it our own self-destructive theology.

"The thief comes to steal, kill, and destroy, but <u>I have come to</u> <u>give life and life abundantly.</u>" ~Jesus Christ (see John 10:10)

As I think of Jesus' declaration, I can't help but think of *anything* that comes to destroy our God-given dreams and desires as being *anti-Christ* and straight up *satanic*. I want to encourage you to reject any form of pump-you-up sermons that are only a veiled way of telling you to *die again* the death that Jesus died for you. Don't spend time killing off the life Jesus gave you.

There's a word for that—*Gnosticism* (go look it up).

All of these passages were never meant to become self-denial passages that make people think they need to quit doing the things they love. The only *self* that you need to deny is the *old-selfish-sinful-self* that has now been dead and buried through the death of Christ on the cross.

Your dreams and desires are not to be put to death. Those are things that Jesus put in you. Sure, keep them surrendered to Him just as your very life is no longer your own (1 John 4:17, Galatians 2:20, 2 Corinthians 5:16). But please, feel the freedom to make tons of cash, have an amazing family, get a great job, serve the poor, play sports, write books, go to parties, and enjoy your life!

Trust me, the world *and the church* will pass out enough persecution and hardship for you; there's no need to bring it on yourself through your mindset of self-loathing. *Go, live life and live it to the fullest!!!*

CHAPTER 4
THE POINT OF EVERYTHING
Togetherness

I think it was Socrates that asked the question…or maybe Plato.

Or maybe it was the 4 year old playing with Play-Dough.

Or maybe all of them…or all of *us* at one point in time.

"What is the meaning of life?"

You've got to love it when folks say the most profound things that everyone else is already thinking (and saying) and then try to turn it into a quote.

But, *whatever*. I'm sure I've done it, too. Heck, I'm probably doing it right now (thus, this book).

So, I'll pretend like I came up with this question and ask it again, very *profoundly*…

"What is the meaning of life?"

I'm not going to answer this question perfectly. Honestly, I hope you're not expecting to get that answer from me. But I will start a conversation that will get us all thinking and hopefully bring us closer to our divine origin and our eternal purpose.

Remember the first time you realized that you had one of the characteristics of your Mom or Dad? I do. I think I was about 28 or 29 years old when I noticed the way I walked and talked was almost exactly like my Dad. It's something you try to deny, if you're someone who fights for *uniqueness,* but it's something that's true about all of us, regardless of whether we realize it or not.

The more I have gotten to know my Dad—who is an amazing guy—the more I've actually become aware of who I am and where I come from. Something about familiarity breeds comfort in the heart. This is how family was created to be.

In the same way, we all have the longing to know *where we came from* and *who we came from.* Don't worry, I'm not going to try to become a philosopher, I'm just laying a foundation for one of the simplest yet most profound subjects that we could talk about—*our origin and our purpose.*

Beer and cigars were created for topics such as these. So kick back, let's enjoy a good conversation about the *purpose of everything* ☺

THE THEOLOGY OF A 5th GRADER

Growing up in a Christian home down in the South, I found myself at Church every Sunday morning and almost every Wednesday evening. I became very accustomed to the Bible and could tell you all kinds of great stories from it. I was a pretty innocent, open-minded, and humble kid.

I was yet to realize that this wonderful book called "The Bible" had been used to divide, demean, and conquer smaller and weaker people as well as to bring light and hope to many. All I knew was that this book was about the God who loved me and the God who loved *everyone*.

I remember sitting in my Presbyterian private school at the age of ten when a very interesting conversation came up. Little did I know the theological implications of such a conversation. Somehow we went from math to talking about God (that's private school for ya).

The teacher, in her mid-twenties, proceeded to talk about how God loves some people and hates other people. I was so confused. Leave it to a kid to think he knows theology before he's ever studied it. *Imagine that, a kid actually thinking that he knows God.* Well, I sure thought I did, enough so to chime in during the conversation and tell Ms. Smith that she was wrong.

"I think God loves everyone," I said with a rather concerned and serious tone.

That was all it took. I remember her taking a moment to stare into the carpet with an intrigued look on her face and saying something like, *"Hmmm…I'll have to think about that."*

Really?
You'll have to think about that?

I was a 10-year old kid who pretty much just knew that somewhere in John 3 it said God loved the world. I couldn't break down all of the biblical interpretation of verses that seemed to say differently, but I knew one thing, **God is love**. And if everyone is *not* included in that love, then who in the world was this "god" we said we believed in?

I am reminded of the famous movie "Forrest Gump" (a great flick to us 30-something's and a *Turner Classic Movie* to the 20 year olds). In the movie, a mentally challenged adult, Forrest Gump, falls in love with a beautiful young lady, Jenny, who befriended him as a child. At one point Jenny looks at Forrest as he try's to declare his undying love for her, and she says, *"Forrest, how would you know what love is?"*

Forrest, with an exasperated yet focused look on his face, says, *"Jenny, I'm not a smart man, but I know what love is."* This is the same feeling that I felt as a 10-year old in my 5th grade class. I may not have had all of the answers, but I knew God loved people. And hey, this is why Jesus said that the Kingdom was made for these little guys; because they have yet to unlearn love through broken men's theology.

FRIENDS OR ENEMIES?

Jesus said that there was no greater love than this: that one would lay down His life for His *friends*. I find it rather interesting that Christ Himself calls us His friends and the Apostle Paul said something almost seemingly opposite,

"But God demonstrates His own love toward us, in that while we were yet sinners, Christ died for us. 10 For if while we were enemies we were reconciled to God through the death of His Son, much more, having been reconciled, we shall be saved by His life." Romans 5:8, 10 (NASB)

In these verses Paul says that while we were *enemies*, Christ died for us and *reconciled us* to God. In Matthew Jesus says He died for

His friends.

So were we His *friends* or His *enemies?*

Well, in our minds we were enemies (Colossians 1:21) but in His mind, we were His friends all along.

Knowing that the world was literally in opposition to Him, Jesus still called us *friends*. While we were still enemies of God *in our minds,* Christ died for us and showed us that we were *His friends.*

It's like the son who ran from his father because he thought he knew better than his own Dad. He thought his dad was against him and wanted to withhold good things from him. So he ran from his dad and used every good thing his Dad provided for him as a means to do the opposite of what he was taught. He left home, lived a wild and crazy lifestyle, and all the while, the Father sat at home waiting for his son, his *friend* to return home and enjoy fellowship with him.

Was his Dad ever **angry** or **frustrated**? It is definitely probable. But his anger or frustration was never shown to be detrimental to the wellbeing of the son nor did the son's disobedience ever negate his son-ship. Dad's frustration was based in a broken heart but tempered by the hope of knowing his son would be restored completely.

When Christ died for humanity, He didn't only die for those who He knew would eventually *believe* in His death for them. He died for all mankind—everyone.

EXPERTS AT EXCLUSION

Humanity has always found a way to choose one and exclude the other.

Rewarding *the good*
and
punishing *the bad*.

God, on the other hand, is not looking at humanity through the eyes of *separation* and *exclusion*.

He doesn't see American and European, African and Asian, Hindu and Muslim, Christian and Buddhist. God sees HUMANITY.

Traditional Evangelicalism has demanded that we create divisions and separations. Whether they are political, national, or religious, we really *love* our dividing lines.

They keep us comfortable.

Labels and distinctions keep us *safe* and *secure*. They're necessary so that we all know who is *right* and who is *wrong…right?*

The message about God the majority of the world has heard is about a God of exclusion and separation.

There seems to be this idea that *God hates people* until they *believe in Him.*

Well, what exactly are they supposed to *believe about Him?*

"That He loved them enough to die on the cross for their sins, of course."

So let me get this right…

God *hates people* until people believe that God *loves them.* Once people believe that God *loves them,* He then stops *hating them,* and starts *loving them*?

Or how about this one...

If God is for us then who can be against us? (Romans 8:39)

Who is the "*us*" in this passage? How do we become one of those included in this *us* group? "*Well, we have to believe that it's true about us in order for it to be true about us,*" some would say. So, God is *for us* when we **believe** that He is *for us*? And before we *believe* it, God is against us? Does anyone else see a problem with this?

Romans 5 is the passage preceding this verse. It declares that God was *for everyone,* and that's why He came and gave His life on our behalf — while we were still *against Him.*

The Pagans. Secularists. Muslims. Hindus. Humanists. New-agers. Homosexuals. We like to imagine that God is **against these people.** This gives us, Christians, a reason to be against them.

Of course, we say we aren't against *the people.* We are only against *their ideologies.* Unfortunately, it comes across much differently to a world that is waiting to see what God actually looks like.

Inevitably, we become what we worship. If we worship a God who is angry at humanity until they *get their act together,* then we will also be angry at people until they change. We will approach people in order to *change them* instead of to love and enjoy them. This is something that Jesus never did and never does. If Jesus waited for us to believe in His love *before* He loved us, then we'd all be in big trouble.

What if God is **not against humanity?** What if God **loves everyone?** What if Jesus cared about everyone regardless of what they believed about Him? What if God's love was unconditional?

If you're like me, those questions put a smile on my face. I can't say that I've always been open to asking those questions, but that's part of growing and maturing…

Some of these thoughts are already stretching many of you. I commend you for being open to change and open to growth.

You and I both are still growing and still learning. So let's hold on tight and keep reading, because the good news gets even better.

WHO'S YOUR DADDY?

I love the story of the Prodigal Son.

You know, the story of the son who demanded his inheritance from his Father then ran off and wasted it on cars, porn, prostitutes, and alcohol. Well, I've all too often heard preachers say that this story is about that "backslidden Christian" who needs to "come on home to the Father tonight." And, of course, at the end of the sermon, dozens of young people come streaming forward to *rededicate* their lives to Jesus.

Don't get me wrong, that's fine and dandy, and I'm thankful that Jesus is preached. But all too often these kids just end up back in their so called "backslidden" lifestyles waiting for the next *revival service* to come around so they can pray that prayer again and "get right" with God one more time.

I used to preach the "Prodigal Son = Backslidden Christian" message too… well, that was until I realized that when Jesus shared this story, there was no such thing as a Christian (much less, a *backslidden* one). Actually, it seems that pretty much nobody believed in Jesus while He was here. I mean, yeah, of course His disciples *followed* Him, but did they really *believe* His message? Or much less, *even understand it?* Actually, it seems that they almost all ditched Him in His finest hour. Back to the prodigal son story…

For some reason the church tends to think that they are the son that Jesus was talking about; that we were the ones who were "in" and *the rest of the world (those unbelieving outsiders)* are nowhere to be found in this story. I can't help but see the attitude of the church lining up more with the *older brother* in the story instead of the young prodigal. I guess we'll have to start at the beginning if we're ever going to get any clarity on who's in and who's out— who's God's kid and who's a reprobate bastard.

Christians are experts at coming up with *systems, formulas, and labels*. Systematic *theology*, formulas for *faith*, and labels for those who *don't agree* with us. All the while forgetting that trying to fit God into a system is like trying to… *wait, there's nothing stupid enough to compare with that.*

Formulas for faith?

Well, that's just foolish.

Labeling others?

That only serves to put a box around them, so we feel comfortable shutting them out. Not to mention it gives us a filter through which to listen to them.

What if God wasn't *up in heaven* looking at humanity as a divided family? What if from His vantage point, we were one?

R e l a x ….

I know that not everyone *believes* the same exact thing. But just because one of the kids in the family runs away from home doesn't mean that we are not all in the same family. It just means that kid needs to get fresh perspective of how great his parents are. Now, that's easy when you've got great parents *and* great brothers and sisters.

But when the parents want you home, but your brothers and sisters shun you for your mistakes and wrong thinking and say that you are *not a part of the family until you "make things right,"* then that is definitely not very inviting. You already feel like trash, and they are just confirming your feelings of anti-belonging.

Let's dream together.

What if the Father accepted the son *as a son* even while he wasn't *believing* like a son or *acting* like a son? According to Jesus, that seems to be the case.

Back to the story... [sigh]...thank you for your patience; I chase rabbits as a side-hobby.

When that young son came groveling home on that bright sunny morning in July, he was fully expecting to give a speech of repentance and remorse while receiving a new role as a slave in the family. When he got home, he was hardly able to get past the *"Hey Dad...sorry I screwed everything up,"* when his Dad told him to shut up and gave him a huge hug!

The son wanted to tell his Dad that he'd be sleeping in the barn tonight when suddenly Dad told him to head upstairs, and the servants would be getting his clothes ready for the party. The entire neighborhood was invited. Dad pulled out his debit card and gave it to the servant, telling him to go buy everything needed for a massive celebration—*"and don't hold back on your spending; I want the best of everything for tonight,"* he demanded with a smile on his face.

Everyone came that night. It was wild—literally the biggest party the city had ever seen. Dad pulled out all the stops that night.

Gave the kid a new wardrobe, upgraded his living situation at the house, surprised him with a Z-3, and told him he'd be taking the week off of work to spend some quality time with him. Everyone had a blast, and they were all so grateful for the return of the son. Well, everyone except his older brother.

He left the party early and went to hang out in the basement, pouting and watching reruns of *Full House* on *Netflix*. When Dad noticed he wasn't around, he searched the house until he found him in the basement.

"*Buddy!*" Dad said with a smile, (he had called him by this nickname since he was a kid). "*You're missing all the action! Besides, you never hang down here… What's up?*"

The older brother didn't take his eyes off of the Flat-Screen,

"*Dad, seriously? The Z3? A party? New wardrobe? What the heck is going on?!?*" the brother asked with disdain. "*Never once have I gotten a party this big, and never once have you given me half of what you just gave this idiot son of yours. I seriously wonder how you expect to see any change in him if you're just going to reward his stupid behavior like this!*"

Dad cleared his throat and contained himself,

"*Wow, son, I didn't know you felt this way. But, yes, you're right. We really did throw quite the party for this <u>brother of yours</u>,*" he said emphasizing the fact that *they were brothers.*

"*Ya know, bud, you and your brother have been close since you were kids. I really appreciate the way you've loved him and helped him out over the years. We both know that he's always had to learn the hard way in life, but that never made him anything less than a brother to you or a son to me. You both come from me, and nothing you can do can change that. You're my kids and you are brothers.*

Besides that, 'the Z-3?' Are you serious? Dude, you can drive any one of the Beamers or Audi's whenever you feel like it! Just ask. Heck, just go drive 'em. I've always made that clear to you! And if you want to take it with you when you move out, then feel free; it's yours! I mean, honestly, consider it all yours anyway. I trust you and I love you.

Wipe that frown off of your face and come celebrate, Bud! Your brother was practically dead out there on the streets and now he's home. I don't have time to make him feel bad for his decisions. He's been eating with pigs and feeling like one himself. That's enough punishment for one lifetime."

And that's where the story ends. No response given. Not that he didn't respond, but we just don't know how he did.

I think Jesus ended the story like this on purpose. The response is up to the reader. Of course, we all think that we are the prodigal son in this story. And sure, in some way we have all been that son — that's actually the *point* I'm making.

But I don't think it ends there.

I have a feeling that we think we're at the party celebrating the son's homecoming, or our own, but in reality, we are all just hanging out down in the basement with one another watching the 4th series of *Full House*. A *whole notha' pseudo-party* happening downstairs.

The church enjoying the *basement* and the company of other *brothers* while we talk about how loud and blasphemous the party is upstairs. All the while, missing the real party that is actually all about the jacked-up younger brother that we call *"that son of yours."*

*"There's no way that **sinner** is my brother. I want nothing to do with him until he starts representing the family correctly — in his **beliefs** and **actions**."*

Sound familiar?

You might think this example is a little extreme, and I would have to agree. It is extreme. But it's not far-fetched. The church has found an identity in telling the world that they don't belong. I think it's time we find our identity in the God who has redeemed the world with the essence of who He is — LOVE.

JESUS TRIED TO PAY MY PARKING TICKET

I remember when I first moved to Nashville. I moved downtown and lived in a little apartment right in the middle of the city. The area was decent. The parking was less than desirable. Okay, it was *terrible*.

One night I came home around midnight to find that the lot was completely filled. When I checked the street there were "no parking" signs on the meters right outside my building. So I thought, "Well, there is literally nowhere else to park and there are other people parked here...so, what the heck." I parked there.

At 8am I walked out to my car only to find a nice little parking ticket on all of the cars in that lane, including mine. Well, this was my second ticket in 2 weeks since living downtown, so I was a little perturbed. "Oh well," I thought "I'll just pay the ticket and get over it."

I walked in and saw my good friend, Jim, and we started chatting. Jim is a man in his mid-50's who used to be homeless. He's got a heart of gold, but didn't seem to be very open to *God-talk*.

I know this because when I moved in, he immediately started asking me questions about my book and why I was writing about *grace*. I told him I'd give him a copy and let him read it. He said he usually doesn't read that stuff, but maybe he would.

"Did ya see the ticket on your car?" he asked with a smirk on his face.

"Yep, sure did," I answered.

The next he said surprised me…

"Well, if you are strapped for cash and need to pay for other stuff, then let me know. We can help…"

"Oh no, I'm fine," I said. *"It's just fifty bucks. I'll be okay…"*

What? Did he really just offer to pay my parking ticket for me? When I looked into this man's eyes as he offered to pay my ticket, I saw Jesus talking to me. Immediately, my spirit was caught in an inward ecstatic experience. As I walked toward my apartment, I couldn't help feeling that I had just seen Jesus in that man. Yes, that man who really didn't like to talk about *God*.

I remember years ago when I was driving down I-20 in Texas between Dallas and Tyler, I stopped for a homeless man on the side of the Interstate. I mean, I know it can be super dangerous to do that stuff these days, but whatever. I just knew I needed to stop for this guy. When he got in my car, I just remember those beautiful, pure-blue eyes and the big smile he gave me.

I gave him a ride for about 8 miles and dropped him off at a nearby truck stop. As we drove, he started telling me how he wrote songs and poems. He found out I was a minister and so he decided to share a "Christian" song with me. He said it in poem form—a cowboys' version of Jesus.

I have no recollection of the words to that song, but I do remember I felt like I was giving Jesus Himself a ride to the truck stop. I have no clue if the dude was a believer or if he'd ever prayed the *sinner's prayer*. But I know one thing; I saw Christ in this man.

WHO'S HE IN AND WHO'S HE WITH?

As I have watched this awakening of grace stir the pot of the religious system and shake the trash out of the church, I have been more than aware that there are some things that are *okay* to say and other things that are just *not okay*.

Saying that Christ is *in* someone without knowing whether or not they have been *converted to Christianity* or prayed the *sinner's prayer* or *invited Jesus into their hearts* is one of those evangelical no-no's.

But I'm not mostly concerned about what people say is right and wrong, I am interested in what is *true*. Often, I find that folks are taking their system of biblical interpretation from Western tradition instead of actually *rightly dividing* the Scriptures. Many people come to conclusions based upon what they've been told instead of being open to other ideas that are actually found within the Orthodox tradition. This topic (Christ within) is one of those topics that Evangelical culture has *decided upon* regardless of Scriptures that declare a different opinion.

We'll touch on this more a bit later…

Jesus often said things that challenged the religious status quo — the kind of stuff that caused even the best of theologians to squirm. Remember that story He told about the judgment seat? You know, the one where He seems to judge people based upon their treatment of the poor?

34 "Then the King will say to those on His right, 'Come, you who are blessed of My Father, inherit the kingdom prepared for you from the foundation of the world. 35 For I was hungry, and you gave Me something to eat; I was thirsty, and you gave Me something to drink; I was a stranger, and you invited Me in; 36 naked, and you clothed Me; I

was sick, and you visited Me; I was in prison, and you came to Me.'
37 Then the righteous will answer Him, 'Lord, when did we see You
hungry, and feed You, or thirsty, and give You something to drink?
38 And when did we see You a stranger, and invite You in, or naked,
and clothe You? 39 When did we see You sick, or in prison, and come to
You?' 40 The King will answer and say to them, 'Truly I say to you, to
the extent that you did it to one of these brothers of Mine, even the least
of them, you did it to Me.'" Matthew 24:34-41 (NASB)

By the end of this story, Jesus leaves us with no other option
except the fact that whatever we do to *anyone* we are basically
doing it to Him. Well, why is that? Because Christ is the origin of
man and has forever bound Himself to every single one of us.

Most families I know have that one sibling who is a little different
than the rest of the family. The *black sheep*, if you will. Some are
worse than others, but most families have them. Imagine that your
brother, the black sheep, abandons your family and treats you all
like trash.

Even though he is being a complete idiot, it doesn't change the
fact that he came from your mother and father. As much as the
mother and father would like to just let it go and forget about him,
they can't. He is forever bound to them by name and by blood.

When you hear of someone treating your black sheep brother or
son in a disrespectful manner, you take it personally. Regardless
of how rude he's been to you, you still stand up for him. Why?

Because he is family.

In the same way, when someone treats your family well, you take
it personally.

That's why we say things like, *"Any friend of (insert name of favorite*
sibling here) is a friend of mine!"

Jesus is the same way with *all of humanity*. He experiences the joy of the homeless man who receives a hug from the selfless rich dude. He also experiences the pain of a wealthy man who feels isolated and alone. He experiences the joy and pain of all humanity and knows everyone individually and intimately whether they know it or not.

When an unbeliever is treated like less than human because of their belief system, Jesus *feels* their pain. When believers are persecuted for her faith, Jesus *feels* their pain. It all matters in His eyes.

GOD, THE FATHER OF CRACK ADDICTS

Last week I walked out of a church called *The Anchor* in downtown Nashville and ran into a homeless man named *Alvin*. I walked right up to him and asked him how he was doing and what he needed. He told me he hadn't eaten in two days and needed some money.

Of course, I have no idea if his story was true or not, but I just looked at him in the eyes, introduced myself to him and told him that he was amazing. I walked with him to my car and took him to the local gas station. On the way, I began to tell him that I have big hopes for his life and I see a good future for him.

He told me that his parents were drug addicts and he is really struggling. He opened up and got really honest with me and told me that he's been doing drugs too.

I knew that was probably the case.

But I decided I wouldn't treat him according to that identity but instead see the *God-potential* within him and speak the truth to him, even if we only had a few minutes together. I went to the gas station and got some cash out of the ATM, not knowing what he'd use it for.

I walked over and gave it to him, and he quickly stuffed it into his left shoe. He was very paranoid and would hardly look me in the eye, so finally I said, *"Alvin, I need you to look me in the eye so that I can have the opportunity to tell you…"*

He looked up fearfully…

"…that you are absolutely amazing and I am proud of you."

He lit up with the biggest smile I've ever seen.

Then he gave me a hug. I told him I loved him and I believe in him. I told him that Jesus died for his sins and he is forgiven of all the bad stuff he's done. I told him that God loves him, and anytime he needs Him, just to say His name, *"Jesus."*

We parted ways and I know that Alvin probably was going to grab some alcohol, but I knew that I had just appealed to the truth of who God had called Alvin to be from the foundation of the world and I knew Alvin's spirit could taste the truth, and he would probably never forget it.

I saw within Alvin, the truth of the God-life hidden within. I could see the value of a *life created by God and born from above.*

I could see within Alvin's joyful eyes, the life of Christ that sustains and upholds his every breath. I treated Alvin based upon that truth and not based upon how crazy he had been acting.

My job was not to convince Alvin to change. My job was to love Alvin genuinely and without expectation.

Love without conditions. Care without qualifications.

What if we did this to everyone we met?

What if we treated them like we were literally running into *Jesus Himself?*

Alvin is a son of God. He comes straight from God and God has never left him.

There's a story in the bible (Acts 17) about the Apostle Paul coming to folks in Athens and speaking to them about God's love for them. He didn't come to them telling them how bad they were and how they needed to quickly stop sinning or they would burn in hell. In fact, he didn't even *mention hell.*

Instead, Paul told them they were children of God and they came from God. Paul told these *unbelievers* they were the offspring of God and they were *in Him.*

He went on to tell them God has chosen to judge all mankind in the Person of Jesus Christ and this judgment was sure. He judged mankind righteous in Christ and proved this through Christ's resurrection from the dead.

It's interesting to look at the actual *Greek words* that Paul used when speaking to the Athenians at Mars Hill.

He told them, *"God has appointed a day in which he will judge the world in righteousness by that man whom He has ordained."*

The phrase *"he will"* (*judge*) is actually the word μλλω (*mellō*) in the Greek.

It is in the *present active* tense.

So what's the big deal? We all know that judgment day *is coming,* and that's all that Paul is trying to tell these guys here, *right?*

Well, maybe not. The verb tense is important.

Actually, it's <u>very important</u>.

Could it be that Greek to English bible translators have missed it on this one? Well, it wouldn't be the first time.

Look at the verb tense in these two examples and tell me if the tense is not important…

Graduation Day is coming soon, so you better work hard to get your degree so that you will eventually have your credentials to get a good job.

Vs.

Graduation Day *is here,* and you have passed with flying colors. Go and get a killer job based on the fact you now *have the credentials.*

"The present tense represents a simple statement of fact or reality viewed as occurring in actual time. In most cases this corresponds directly with the English present tense.

Some phrases which might be rendered as past tense in English will often occur in the present tense in Greek. These are termed "historical presents," and such occurrences dramatize the event described as if the reader were there watching the event occur. Some English translations render such historical presents in the English past tense, while others permit the tense to remain in the present." (blueletterbible.org)

I love the way Francois Du Toit translates this section of Scripture in his widely talked about *Mirror Translation:*

"because God had fixed a day on which he would judge the world righteous by a man whom he has appointed, and of this he has given proof to all mankind by raising him from the dead…" Acts 17:29-31 The Mirror Translation

Christ has done the job for mankind, and Paul was declaring what Christ had done for us all. After he spoke this message to the unbelievers at Mars Hill, some were intrigued and wanted to hear more, and some thought he was crazy.

What was Paul's reaction to their rejection?

Nothing.

Did he freak out and tell them they better hurry up and *believe* or they would burn?

Did he tell them that the *wrath of God* was on their trail, and they better quickly say the *sinners prayer?*

Nope. None of that.

He didn't do any of that.

And I have been intrigued by this even to the point of frustration. If Paul didn't do this, then why does the evangelical church do it?

"But didn't he say that God commands all men to repent?"

Of course he did! But *repent* is not a scary word. And neither is *command.*

In fact, in the Greek, the first transliteration for the word *command* means *to announce!*

And our English word *repent* comes from the Greek word *metanoia* which means to *"change one's mind"* and to *"come to the knowledge of the truth."*

The work that Christ has done is so wonderful that God announces to all men that we should *change our minds (repent)* and live in light of this truth! He desires that none would continue to live in the deathly slumber of unbelief but that everyone would awaken to the reality of God's love for them and their inclusion in what Christ has done for them on the cross.

Paul's declaration of the *pagan's* inclusion in the righteousness of

God is scandalous. But it makes sense. That's the good news... God did for you what you couldn't do for yourself, based upon His righteousness not upon yours. Your enjoyment of the gift happens when you lay down your own efforts to include yourself and trust in what He has done for you!

THE "BAD GUYS" WHO DO GOOD STUFF

Jesus told a story that has been popularized in Christian culture by the name *"The Good Samaritan."* I never quite realized how scandalous this story must've been to those Jewish boys and girls who were listening to Jesus that day.

Those folks grew up hearing about the *bad Samaritans* down the road and how they were all *going to be destroyed by God* because they were so evil. These Samaritans were basically *half-Jews* who didn't follow the customs of the Hebrews. They were the *untouchables*, the *unclean*, and the *outcasts* of society.

This was the reason Jesus was looked at as strange for having spoken to the woman at the well. She was a **Samaritan** and a *woman*. Both of these things played against her in the social scheme.

Back to the *story...*

It was quite awkward for Jesus to put a Samaritan in his story and paint a *good* picture of him.

The story begins with a man walking on a journey in the backwoods. On his way to the nearest city, the man gets robbed and beaten up by some hood-rats and is then left for dead. While lying half-dead on the road, three men end up coming upon him. First is the Rabbi. This teacher was in a hurry and had to get to his ministry meeting, so he had no time to stop to help this bloodied man.

Next was a Levite; a good Israel-loving-conservative Levite. He was on his way to a meeting as well and definitely had no time to stop and check on this man.

So, he also passed right by the half-dead man.

The dude, still laying there bloodied and beaten, decided he'd just give up and die.

I mean, if a *Spirit-led* **Levite**

and a **pious Pastor** *(rabbi)* from the local synagogue

wouldn't stop to help,

then **no one** would.

As he pondered his last breaths, he was suddenly startled by a man stooping over him. "Are you okay?" said the man as he reached down to pick up the cripple.

Stunned, the little Jewish man realized it was a Samaritan who was reaching over to pick him up.

"How could this be?" he thought to himself.

"Dad always told me these guys were jerks."

Well, it turns out this Samaritan put the guy on his donkey and rode him to the nearest hotel. He put the guy up in a nice room and called the hospital. This ole' Samaritan paid his two week hospital bill as well as his hotel stay.

Can you imagine the mixed reactions of the crowd Jesus was speaking to?

"No way! Not a dirty-Samaritan!"

"Hmmm...I never woulda' thought..."

"Wow... I knew those guys weren't so bad!"

Jesus knew all the buttons to push. So he went after their deepest prejudice. And kicked it where it hurt...

"Love your neighbor as yourself," was the command that preceded this story. And, of course, he ended the story with this question: *"Who showed mercy to the man?"* In other words, *"Who fulfilled the command I just gave? Who, in this story, LOVED?"*

The answer was obvious, yet a little disconcerting. In essence, what Jesus had just said was this:

*"The 'unclean' Samaritan just expressed the love of God to this man. He just treated this person as His neighbor the same way God treats **everyone** as His neighbor.*

Yes, the Samaritan who you are convinced is utterly depraved and can do no good, he is the one who expressed the fragrance of My Father.

So, go and act like a Samaritan."

I have a feeling this is not hitting home with us. To make the story a little more relevant, just substitute the following characters and reread the story:

Rabbi – *Local Pastor*

Levite – *Worship leader*

Samaritan – *Liberal voting Transvestite*

Now that's better ☺

For some of you, that's not a big deal. But for those of you who have grown up in the world of the evangelical church, you know the implications of such a statement.

"So Blaise, what are you trying to say?"

What I am *trying to say* is that God's love, character, and nature is able to shine through those whom Christians often discount as dirty, sinful, and completely "unredeemed."

God's imprint and image remain on every human being and shines through them regardless of their awareness of it.

Look at Jesus' response to the Pharisees in Luke 20…

21 *They questioned Him, saying, "Teacher, we know that You speak and teach correctly, and You are not partial to any, but teach the way of God in truth.* **22** *Is it lawful for us to pay taxes to Caesar, or not?"* **23** *But He detected their trickery and said to them,* **24** *"Show Me a denarius. Whose likeness and inscription does it have?" They said, "Caesar's."* **25** *And He said to them, "Then render to Caesar the things that are Caesar's, and* **to God the things that are God's***."* Luke 20:21-25 (ESV)

Jesus seems to always answer questions with even better questions. The key to understanding Jesus' final answer about the coin actually lies in understanding his question to the Pharisees: *whose* **image** *is on the coin?*

These guys had no idea where Jesus was going with this. They went ahead and answered Him, *"Caesar's, of course."*

"Well," said Jesus, *"if Caesar's image is on the coin then let's give it to him. Oh, and by the way,* God's image is on your life*; so make sure to give that back to Him."*

Jesus made that declaration about

***Every human being* on the planet.**

Knowing that the Pharisees were plotting to kill God in flesh, Jesus made the audacious declaration that these guys bore the perfect image of God. Regardless of their inadequate expression of

God's character and nature at that moment, they still bore His image and belonged to Him. You might mar the image, but nonetheless, the image remains.

FRIENDSHIP

So... remember, I am a rabbit-chaser.

I'm still answering the greatest question in all of our minds: *what is the point of life?* I just like to build a case. Thanks for hanging in there ☺

From the very beginning God had one thing in mind for mankind: **friendship**. When God created Adam, He put him in the middle of a bunch of animals. After a certain amount of time, it became clear to Adam that he wasn't going to be having any good fellowship with these guys. I like to imagine that these animals could talk before "the fall." But, regardless, they weren't going to be having the kind of fellowship that two humans could have with one another.

The Lord saw that there was no one *comparable* to Adam, so He made Adam a friend. He created *Eve* in Adam's image and likeness. True fellowship requires image equality.

In the same way that Adam needed God, God *needed* Adam.

Don't freak out. I know that God didn't *need anything*.

God wanted — *deeply desired* — Adam's fellowship. The Father, Son, and Spirit looked at One another and said, *"Hey, Let's make someone who is exactly like Us — in our image and likeness. Let's make him so he'll be able to enjoy constant fellowship and friendship with Us. Let's make someone we can hang out with, walk through the garden with, and enjoy on deep levels of friendship."*

So They did.

God created Adam and Eve. He walked with them in the garden and enjoyed fellowship with them.

Of course, you know the story... they totally screwed up the relationship, believed the lie, and hid from God. The crazy part about this story is God's reaction to their *screw up*. It seems like most folks interpret God's *"Adam, where are you?"* in the harshest tone possible. It seems that we have an innate sense that God is always angry at Adam and can't wait to kick him out of the garden and pronounce a curse on him.

Well, I have some surprising news for you: **Adam's sin didn't change God's mind about him.**

Adam's sin didn't catch God by surprise. You see, before Adam disobeyed God, God had a plan of forgiveness and redemption already in place. In fact, God's redemption plan was as good as done. Let me go even further to say that Adam's sin *did not separate him from God.*

Yes, I just said that.

Adam was only separated from God *in his own mind*. God has no problem approaching people in their sin. In fact, He's un-phased by sin in regards to His ability to love someone. The problem of sin is that it *distorts our view of ourselves and our view of God.*

Look what Paul said to the Colossians (1:21) about sin's distorting power:

*"And although you were formerly alienated and **hostile in mind**, engaged in evil deeds,"* (NASB)

*"And you, who once were alienated **and enemies in mind by wicked works**, yet now has it reconciled,"* (Darby)

*"And you, being in time past alienated and **enemies in your mind in your evil works"** (ASV)*

*"You, too, were once estranged from him; **your minds were alienated from him by a life of sin,"** (Knox)*

God was *never our enemy,* and we were never *His enemy.* But something happened *in our minds* when we believed the lie of the devil. What was this lie? It was the accusation that God was not good and had not provided everything we needed.

"God knows if you eat of this tree, then you will be like Him," was the accusation of the devil.

But the problem was they were already *like Him.* That's how He created them—in His image and in His likeness.

Temptations from the enemy always find their root in this lie: *you need to do something **more** in order to become something **more** because obviously God has been withholding something from you.*

This lie got into their heads, and they did the first *evil deed.* It wasn't a murder or a rape. It wasn't even a theft or a lie. It was simply eating from the tree of the knowledge of good and evil. And this is the last thing God wanted them to do.

God's intention for mankind was that we would never eat from the tree of the knowledge of good *and* evil. That *knowledge* is what much of the church and religions of the world are still eating from today, and it's produced nothing but death and destruction.

God didn't want us awakened to a false knowledge that had to do with trying to do right and avoid wrong. God's intention was that we would *only* eat from the tree of life that would *only* enhance our understanding of our identity as His sons and daughters.

Today, religion teaches we've got to *do right* in order to *be right* and we have to *avoid wrong* in order to *stay right*. It's still a man-centered message that says *we* have the power to *make ourselves* into something. When we reject that old tree and start eating from the Tree of Life, then we are strengthened in the truth of our sonship, and we live with our minds so engulfed in the truth that the lie becomes a laughable mirage.

The true Tree of Life is Jesus Christ. Knowing Him is eternal life (John 17:3). In partaking of the truth about Christ, we also partake of the truth about ourselves. Our life is hidden with Christ deeply inside the heart of God (see Colossians 3:3).

When we meet Jesus, it's like meeting ourselves for the first time.

Partaking of the truth about Him causes the lie to fade away. The lie says that God is not *for* us, but that He is *against* us. The lie produces fear that God is out to get us and wants to punish us when we make a mistake.

That's why Adam hid!

He thought God's wrath was coming against Him.

When actually, God's kindness was after him!

"Adam, where are you?" was a question for Adam's sake not for God's.

Where was Adam? He was hiding from the God who loved him. Through this hiding, he declared he was *afraid of God* and believed God *was his enemy*. What was the truth? God was **not** his enemy, and God was not someone for Adam to hide from.

But this is the power of sin.

It's a cycle.

We believe the lie so we do the *sinful deed*.

Then the deed produces in us **fear** that God is going to punish us.

So we hide from the only solution to our problem: God.

Of course, that *fear and condemnation* only ends up producing *more evil deeds*. **So the cycle continues.**

It seems that humanity is in the same predicament as Adam. And the church is not helping the situation. Instead of declaring the God who loves humanity, we often warn people about the God who is angry with them until they fix themselves and *get right with Him*.

The power of sin has tainted the minds of man about ***who*** they are and **Whose** they are.

Everyone, everywhere comes from the same source and is cut from the same rug. *"Look to the rock from which you were cut, And to the quarry from which you were dug,"* says Isaiah the Prophet.

Simply put,

"Hey guys! Don't forget where you came from!

That's where you'll find your source and true identity!"

THE FALL DIDN'T SCREW UP GOD'S PLAN

Somewhere along the way, we got this strange idea that when Adam *sinned* the heavens were shut up, and God turned to cosmic bowling and star-gazing.

"Well, I guess I'll have to wait about 4,000 years until Jesus dies for them so I can be friends with them again."

This was not the case.

Before we fell in Adam, we were found in Christ. God didn't see Adam's sin and say, *"Oh crap. Well, back to the drawing board, boys."*

No, His plans were not thwarted. Even though Adam's mind was tainted with sin and deception, God was still closer than the air Adam breathed, and he still bore God's image. Look what God said after the fall and before the coming of Christ:

"...for in the image of God has God made mankind." Genesis 9:6 (NIV)

The fall didn't change God's view of man, but it changed man's view of God — and of himself.

God had no problem loving mankind all the way through. He was obviously available to anyone at any time. We find that before Moses brought the Law, there were many people who *found God* — or rather, realized that He was never gone to begin with. There were other folks who seemed to realize God's love and kindness towards them before it had been clearly revealed in Christ.

For example, Enoch seemed to walk with God in a pretty intimate way. Abraham and Elijah did similarly. David is one of my favorites. After his six month season of sin, he repented by saying, *"God, I know You got me out of that sinful season and brought me back to you because You enjoy me so much,"* (see Psalm 18:19). This guy knew something about God that many people had lost.

Each one of these guys seemed to pass through the veil of Old Covenant thinking and find that, all along, their sin was not the main issue, but it was their view of God. While many were still trying to appease God through rituals and rules, these guys realized that God already liked them and that He still wanted friendship with them. He was **not their enemy**.

As Francois Du Toit has said so well, *"Before we were lost in Adam, we were found in Christ."*

Through Christ, God has shown that mankind has always been in His heart. There was never a time when God desired to be God apart from mankind. His becoming a man in Christ confirmed that mankind's origin was not in the fall of Adam but in the position of Christ—at the right hand of God.

Our fall was great, but His redemption was greater. Your identity is not in what you've done or what others say about you. Your identity is found in Christ and Christ alone, what He has done for you and what He has said about you.

His declaration about mankind from the beginning was *"he is very good,"* (see Genesis 1:31).

Our sin didn't reverse this declaration in God's mind. It was only in our minds. Our fall didn't cause God to back away from us; it only caused us to turn our backs on Him. Even still, He loves each and every one of us and desires that *all men* would come to the knowledge of the truth (1 Timothy 2:4).

What truth?

The truth of His love for us.

Every person on the face of the planet was created by Him and for Him. God didn't create some for His pleasure and some for His *displeasure*. Instead, all men were created to bring Him joy and pleasure. Look at what Revelation 4:11 says about God's purpose in creating the world…

"You created all things, and because of Your will they existed, and were created." Revelation 4:11 (NASB)

I absolutely love the way the World English Bible translates this in

Revelation 4:11. I believe it catches the heart of the message. Contrary to popular opinion, it was not through a stoic *will* that God created the world, but it was because of His *desire*. God always has and always will be a God of *pleasure* and a God of *desire*.

"You created all things, and <u>because of your desire</u> they existed, and were created!" Revelation 4:11 (WEB)

God's will from the very beginning was to create for His enjoyment and for His pleasure. And of course, the crown of that creation was and still is His children — the ones who are made in His image — that is, **all of humanity.**

We all know we are made for *relationship*. That's why we like to be **together** during the most important times in life. None of us enjoy being alone. There is a true sense of **togetherness** we all enjoy.

I believe it's because we were made for this.

Together with God.

Together with one another.

Found in Him. As a family.

And this **togetherness** is the answer to life's deepest questions.

Not that we come to perfect conclusions, but we go on the journey **together.**

Maybe the entire point of existence is to be **together**, as one, with God and with one another — learning from one another about what is most important. And maybe what is most important is not the **answers** but **the journey. TOGETHER.**

CHAPTER 5
THE DAY GOD THREW A KEG-PARTY
I promise, God doesn't want to kill you!

As I've looked back at the main teachings in the evangelical Church, I can't help but feel like God is being presented as a bit schizophrenic.

"God loves you," and "You better get right with Him or you'll go to hell," and "God wants the best for your life," and "Oh, you had a tire blow out while driving? God must be trying to teach you a lesson."

The contradiction of the God who was angry at people and the God who loved people was hard to come to terms with. Reconciling the God who loved me and the God who may or may not be causing damage to my life was *interesting*, to say the least.

As a young believer, I didn't know what else to do with the contradictions, so I just believed them and went on trusting God. *"Even if He gets a little angry and even mean sometimes,"* I reasoned, *"I'll still trust Him and love Him."* Sure, I'm glad I didn't run off into Satanism or something, but honestly, it might have done me well to at least question some of these conclusions about God.

At times, it seems that the god who is preached from some of the pulpits of America is more like *Zeus*, or even *Satan himself*, than Jesus Christ.

"God's gonna send another tornado because the gays are destroying America."

"God's sending an earthquake to California because of abortion."

"God destroyed your city because of the witchcraft happening there."

"America is under God's judgment because of Hollywood's influence on the world."

I understand there are many Old Testament stories that have to do with God sending *judgment* on a nation or city. But I also know we have a new lens with which to see *God* that the writers of the Old Testament *did not have*.

Before you throw stones, check out some of these verses:

"God, after He spoke long ago to the fathers in the prophets in many portions and in many ways, 2 in these last days has spoken to us in His Son, whom He appointed heir of all things, through whom also He made the world. 3 And He is the radiance of His glory and the exact representation of His nature, and upholds all things by the word of His power." Hebrews 1:1-3a (NASB)

Did I read this correctly? Did he just say that God used to speak through the prophets, *but now* He *has spoken* through Jesus?

What does that mean?

In the past 10 years I have had my times of wanting to be like the Old Testament Prophets. I mean, who wouldn't, right? These guys seemed like they knew God so well, and God trusted them with what He wanted to say to people on the earth.

But as I began reading verses like the one in Hebrews, I began to rethink my desire to be a part of the *Enoch Company* or the *Elijah Generation.* If God spoke *"long ago"* through the Prophets *"but now"* He has spoken to us through Jesus, then I might want to pay more attention to Jesus than I do the Prophets. I know God spoke *through the Prophets,* but it seems like He did something through Jesus Christ that is much more deserving of our attention.

The prophets talked *about* God. Jesus actually *knew* **God**—oh, and don't forget the fact that **He is God.**

Look at this conversation that Jesus had with Phillip:

"Philip said to Him, "Lord, show us the Father, and it is enough for us." 9 Jesus said to him, "Have I been so long with you, and yet you have not come to know Me, Philip? He who has seen Me has seen the Father; how can you say, 'Show us the Father'?" John 14:8-9 (NASB)

If you've been in Church for more than a few weeks, then you've probably heard this Scripture. But in order to feel the *real implications* of what Jesus said here, we've got to go back and look at the context.

What was Jesus actually saying and how did it impact His original audience?

These guys were good Jewish boys who had grown up expecting the Messiah to come and deliver the Jews from Roman rule. They knew the Messiah would be raised up by God, and many even believed he would come directly from heaven (see Daniel 7). But they didn't have much of a grid for this Messiah being equal to God and definitely weren't expecting him to come saying that He **is God**.

This had to freak them out... *at least a little?* Jesus looked at these good Jewish boys and said, *"You guys have been waiting to see **God**, but guess what... here I Am! He is Me and I am Him. We are One and* *have always been One from the beginning. If you've seen Me, then you have seen Him."*

Look at this one from the Apostle John:

"No one has ever seen God, but the one and only Son, who is himself God and is in closest relationship with the Father, has made him known." John 1:18 (NIV)

*"**No one** has ever seen God."* Ummm...John, are you sure about that? I mean, seriously... tons of folks have seen God.

So I guess those guys who lived in the time of the Law and the Prophets who thought they had seen and known Him actually didn't *see* or *know Him.*

Sure, they had a glimpse. But it was just that...

a glimpse.

Look at the time before Jesus came...

Moses saw God on the mountain. Abraham spoke to God like a friend speaks to a friend: face to face. Enoch walked with God (so I assume that he saw Him). I could go on...

"No," says John, "**No one** has seen Him. Jesus is the only One who truly knows Him because He is Him."

Jesus came and showed us something that was not just a *glimpse* but a **perfectly clear representation.**

Jesus Himself has more to say about this...

*"And the Father who sent Me, He has testified of Me. **You have neither heard His voice at any time** nor seen His form." John 5:37 (NASB)*

Again, we have to look at the context.

Jesus is speaking to good Jewish folk who have *definitely heard God's voice* through the Prophets of old. How could this *Jesus* guy come along telling me that I have never heard *God's voice* before? This would be more than disconcerting to me.

This would be devastating.

It's no wonder these guys wanted to crucify him. He basically came along discrediting everything they thought they knew about God and then said he himself *was God.*

If we are going to study the Bible, which I highly recommend, then we should probably do so in context to the Person of Jesus and not through the darkened lenses of Old Covenant Prophets who have never *seen* or *known* GOD.

If Jesus **is God,** then we have a massive problem.

It might mean that some of our theological conclusions were not just a little *off* but altogether stupid. At least, that's what those good Jewish boys and girls realized when they came face to face with the One they knew *everything* about.

RELATIONSHIP STATUS: "IT'S COMPLICATED"

Did you hear about that kid who was "dating" the girl from the *other school?* You know, the kid who said he had a girlfriend that no one really knew. Actually, he had never met her either. She was his online girlfriend who supposedly went to another school.

And she never wanted to see him. But this little middle schooler found her address and went to her house. He texted her and told her to come outside.

She freaked out.

And she came outside. He quickly found out why she never wanted to see him. She was a thirty-five year old woman who had not been taking very good care of herself, to say the least.

Bummer.

We live in such a very different generation. Never before has there been the opportunity to scam one another and pretend like we are someone we are actually not. Social media and online dating, as great as they both are, have created an opportunity for people to *know one another* without actually *knowing one another.*

It's like the guy who is *really interested* in the chic on Facebook for about a year until he actually meets her face to face. If he doesn't light up when he sees her in person, then it doesn't matter how much he knows about her from Facebook. The fact is he really *isn't interested* because he has *no idea* who this person really is.

The folks during Jesus' time ran into this same issue with God. Look what Jesus had to say to them:

"You search the Scriptures, for you believe they give you eternal life. And the Scriptures point to me! **40** *Yet you won't come to me so that I can give you this life eternal!" John 5:39-40 (Living Bible)*

Or how about the Message Bible version:

"You have your heads in your Bibles constantly because you think you'll find eternal life there. But you miss the forest for the trees. These Scriptures are all about me! And here I am, standing right before you, and you aren't willing to receive from me the life you say you want." John 5:39-40 (The Message Bible)

It seems like the relationship was a little complicated for those folks. They all had come to the conclusion that they were on really good terms with God. They knew Him really well because they knew a lot of His history. I'm sure the protests arose after they heard Jesus say this…

*"Come on, Jesus, we know **God** and you are definitely not Him! We have been following Him on Twitter and Instagram for the last 2,000 years and you are definitely not Him."*

It is definitely troublesome when the person whom you think to have the deepest relationship with walks through the room, and you don't even recognize him. This is what was happening to the Jewish folk back then, and this is what is happening to the majority of the Church today.

I wonder what would happen if Jesus (in the flesh) walked right into some of our congregations today. Or what if He attended our afternoon potlucks or our Christian coffee shops?

Would we

even

recognize

Him?

Or would we be a little put off by some of His non-Christian habits and non-Christian friends?

IT SURE WASN'T WELCHES

Jesus had quite the reputation during His time on earth. Growing up, He was a hard worker and a very well respected young man. He honored his parents, worked hard, studied his Torah, and wore his Saturday best to the Temple. We don't hear much about His story from the time He was a boy until he was thirty years old… so we can speculate or we can pick up the story at thirty…

Let's start at 30.

We pick up the story with Him spending time at a local wedding in the city of Cana. It was the third day and, according to the Jewish custom, weddings were seven long days of celebration. Of course, this involved a nice supply of bottomless wine provided by the wedding party.

Unfortunately, halfway through the celebration week, they ran out of the good stuff. Mary, Jesus' mother, came to Him and told him of the dilemma. Let's check out how John records the story:

"On the third day there was a wedding in Cana of Galilee, and the mother of Jesus was there; 2 and both Jesus and His disciples were invited to the wedding. 3 When the wine ran out, the mother of Jesus said to Him, "They have no wine." 4 And Jesus said to her, "Woman, what does that have to do with us? My hour has not yet come." 5 His mother said to the servants, "Whatever He says to you, do it." 6 Now there were six stone water pots set there for the Jewish custom of purification, containing twenty or thirty gallons each. 7 Jesus said to them, "Fill the water pots with water." So they filled them up to the brim. 8 And He said to them, "Draw some out now and take it to the headwaiter." So they took it to him. 9 When the headwaiter tasted the water which had become wine, and did not know where it came from (but the servants who had drawn the water knew), the headwaiter called the bridegroom, 10 and said to him, "Every man serves the good wine first, and when the people have drunk freely, then he serves the poorer wine; but you have kept the good wine until now." 11 This beginning of His signs Jesus did in Cana of Galilee, and manifested His glory, and His disciples believed in Him." John 2:1-11 (NASB)

Don't worry, I'm not going to come up with preacher analogies that will somehow spiritualize this story.

You know... like this:

"Sometimes you feel empty, but Jesus wants to fill you with joy. So, if

you will just fill up your spiritual "water pot" with the water of the Word of God, then the Holy Spirit will come and turn it into the wine of personal revival!"

Wow…that was actually good. I just made that up on the spot.

Anyways… back to the **point** of the story.

Honestly, there is not a deeper meaning to this story. Of course, there are multiple levels of understanding to be gained through meditation and study and God can speak to you personally about the story if He'd like to do so.

But I think we often miss the forest for the trees.

I don't think the Holy Spirit was mainly trying to give us a spiritual lesson about reading our Bibles or praying more. I believe He put this in at the beginning of the letter from John for the sole purpose of showing us one of the most important attributes of God: **FUN.**

God shows up on earth and the first *miracle* that He takes part in has to do with making more *wine* so that people can enjoy the party! Before you choke on your *Testamints (a breath mint sold only at Christian bookstores),* just relax and think about the conclusion of this miracle again.

Jesus is at a wedding celebration when he is told they are almost all out of wine. Obviously there was much more celebrating to be done. He tells them to get six of the 20 gallon buckets and fill them with water. He then proceeds to turn approximately 120 gallons of water into the best alcoholic beverage any of them had tried all week long.

Sorry to break it to all of you good evangelicals, but this was not a *non-alcoholic* beverage.

Welches wasn't invented for another 1,800 years!

Unfortunately, I'm not sure that most Christians would be okay with this miracle if it were to happen today. Could it be that Jesus is more interested in being *human* than he is in being a *Christian?*

What if Jesus, still being fully God, was actually more *normal* than we thought? If His first miraculous act of revealing *His glory* had to do with making a celebration a little livelier, then I have a feeling that we might be on to something here.

JESUS: FRIEND OF THE WEIRD AND NON-WEIRD PEOPLE

Can you imagine a God who is less like your local evangelical neighbor and more like Jesus? That sounds really *neat*, but honestly, which Jesus are we talking about?

Is it the one who is waiting for you to screw up so He can quickly *convict you* of your sins? Is it the Jesus that spends most of His time at political rallies reminding people whom they should and shouldn't vote for? Is it the *Jesus* who is holding *disgusting sinners* over the pit of hell and can't wait to drop them if they don't repent? If that's the *Jesus* we're talking about, then I think I'll pass. And the world has already *passed.*

That's for sure.

So who in the world are we actually talking about? Well, let me share a few thoughts about who *Jesus really is* and what He is really like.

Nowadays, Jesus has a pretty good reputation all across the earth. Even among non-believers, Jesus is a respected person. People usually don't like *Christians,* but they are open to Jesus because He seemed to *do a lot of good.*

Back in the day, the religious folk's view of Jesus was a little different.

*"The Son of Man has come eating and drinking, and you say, 'Behold, a gluttonous man and a drunkard, a **friend of** tax collectors and sinners!'" Luke 7:34 (NASB)*

He enjoyed feasting, He loved a good bottle of wine, and some of His best friends were known as sinners. Jesus loved having **FUN**.

Does anyone else find it strange that the main reputation Christians carry usually has nothing to do with any of those things? Honestly, I'm not telling you that you have to take up *drinking* if you don't want to — that's not the point. And if you love *fasting*, then go on with your hungry self.

But seriously guys, when was the last time you were accused of having too much fun? Or, when was the last time you were accused of having too many *bad friends?* And I don't mean *friends* you only talk to during the *outreach*...

I have a feeling Jesus was not mostly making friends with bad kids just so He could convince them of how bad they were and how good He was.

I think He actually *enjoyed them.*

He wanted to hang out with them because He loved them and saw the beauty of their created value. His love and enjoyment of them (not His preaching) is what actually changed them.

Here's a story to illustrate:

Jesus shows up in town one day, and he is immediately mobbed by the crowd. Everyone was surrounding him hoping for a conversation, a prayer, or an embrace from the man who was transforming the world. Somehow Jesus was able to make everyone feel like the most important person in the world even through a simple glance in their direction. While hugging on the kids and smiling at the widows, he caught a glimpse of a dude hanging out in the trees — literally.

This guy, Zacchaeus, was about 5'5" and couldn't get a good glimpse of Jesus unless he climbed up into the tree — so that's exactly what he did. The rumors of Jesus — his disturbance of the religious system, the miracles he did, and how he was scorned by leaders as a "friend of sinners" — particularly made Zacchaeus curious. Zacchaeus had never been a fan of the religious order, so if there was a dude out there like this, then he had to meet him.

Zacchaeus was a *tax-collector*. This was not a very popular position to hold in the community back then (nor is it today). He definitely used his position and power to make a little extra off of almost everyone he collected from. Actually, let's just shoot straight.

Zack stole from

pretty

much

everyone.

He was straight up gangsta.

Religious leaders wouldn't be caught dead hanging out with a guy like this unless it was for the purpose of telling him how much of an unclean sinner he was. Jesus, on the other hand, saw something completely different about Zack.

While passing by the tree that Zack was hanging in, Jesus called up to him, *"Zacchaeus, dude, come on down! I heard you're having a party at your place tonight!"*

Startled by the attention, Zacchaeus jumped down from the tree,

"What?!? Party? I mean… I…I… wasn't planning one, but I'm sure I could throw something together…"

Jesus laughed as Zack stumbled over his words, and said, *"Yeah, man…party at your place. Invite all of your friends. We're gonna have a feast!"*

Immediately, Zack came down from the tree and with tears in his eyes said,

"Jesus, I would have never imagined you would accept me or pay any attention to me. Today, Lord, I am going to give ½ of everything I own to the poor. And, Lord, if I have stolen anything from anyone in this city, then I am going to pay them back four times as much as I have stolen! Today is a new day, and I feel like myself for the first time in a long time!"

Jesus looked at Zacchaeus. Then He looked at the people *and said,* *"Zacchaeus has been forever changed today, and he's come to understand that he's my kid and not a product of the fallen world."*

No sermon. No picket signs. No declarations of hell and judgment. Zacchaeus was as *saved* as a *saved* person could be. All of this happened because Jesus preached a powerful sermon… in fact it was the shortest and most powerful sermon in all of history.

For you preachers out there, here it is in outline form:

A. Hi Zacchaeus
B. I'm coming to hang out with you

No altar call. No demand to "get right with God." But only an abrupt moment of Jesus *inviting himself over* to the house of a dude who enjoyed stealing from people. This was enough to change this man's life.

Zacchaeus got "saved" because Jesus paid attention to him even though he was a modern day gangster and extortionist. Jesus didn't mention his sin or his need for salvation; Jesus only told him that he wanted to grab dinner with him. He treated Zacchaeus according to his *"before the foundation of the earth"* **identity** and not his current misguided lifestyle.

The sermon was Jesus. The gospel is Jesus. There is no message outside of the Man. Seeing Jesus means seeing the God who is **love incarnate:** Love without expectations; love without demands.

When Jesus sees you, He doesn't see you through the lens of all of your mistakes and problems.

He sees you according to the truth of how He created you.

He sees you as a

child of God.

Jesus doesn't wait until people *get right* with Him before He spends time with us.

If He did that then He never would have come in the first place. The bible says that Jesus is the *friend of sinners* – that means **all of us**. Being a "sinner" is not about how many bad deeds you've done. Being a sinner has to do with being identified with Adam's sin.

That's all there is to it.

We have all been identified with Adam's sin because we were all born from Adam. Jesus didn't reject Adam when he sinned, and Jesus doesn't reject us because of that identification with sin. Instead, He sought out Adam and, in turn, He sought out the entire world. Jesus is mostly interested in the people who think He's not mostly interested in them. That's the point...Jesus came for the ones who actually realize they need Him.

CHAPTER 6
THE ILLUSION OF SEPARATION
Nothing Can Separate You from His Love

"But God demonstrates His own love toward us, in that while we were yet sinners, Christ died for us." Romans 5:8 (NASB)

Somewhere along the way, we got this idea that God is so *holy* He can't be connected to *sinful humanity*. Once I heard about a Charismatic minister who shared a vision he had of Jesus. In this vision he saw Jesus walking up and down the isles of a Church service with His fingers plugging his nose saying, *"Stinking flesh... stinking flesh!"*

Really? Is Jesus really disgusted by *messy* people? Is He really put off by folks who seem a little *imperfect*?

I am all for visions, dreams and heavenly encounters, but when they go directly against the character of God, *or* they are interpreted outside of a New Covenant understanding then they do nothing but damage to the body of Christ.

I don't claim to know whether or not that was a real vision, but I do know one thing. If it *was,* then the folks who heard it misinterpreted it greatly. The only *flesh* Jesus calls *stinking* is the kind that makes us think that we have some part in making ourselves *holy* or keeping ourselves *holy.*

HOLINESS EXPRESSED IN NEARNESS

There's a verse in the Old Testament that seems to give off this idea of God being so *holy* that He can't even *look at our sin.* Check it out:

"Your eyes are too pure to behold evil, and you cannot look on wrongdoing; why do you look on the treacherous, and are silent when the wicked swallow those more righteous than they?" Habakkuk 1:13 (NRSV)

Habakkuk, well intentioned and sincere, still had little understanding of the character and nature of God. Sure, he was a prophet of God. But that doesn't mean he knew God. His confusion is expressed when he asks God about His ability to love, or even look at, sinners,

*"God, You are **too holy** to even look at sinners. So why in the world are you still putting up with them?!?"*

I actually sympathize with Habakkuk. When all you see is *bull crap* happening around you and you, of course, are *keeping your act together* by *living holy,* then it can start to get annoying that God is still *putting up* with all these *sinners.* I definitely have had this mindset before... until I realized that it was wrong.

Interestingly enough, this verse has nothing to do with God being *too holy* to relate to *bad people.* In fact, it actually has more to do with the fact that God *can* and absolutely *does* look upon our sin and is completely undeterred from relating with us.

God is not so clean that He can't get dirty. He's not so *transcendent,* or *far above us* that He has to *look down* in order to see us. In fact, in Christ, God declared that He is Emmanuel, <u>God with Us</u>.

When we think of God, **we must think of Jesus**. There is absolutely no separation between God the Father and the revelation of Jesus in the flesh. Anytime you hear something about God that does not line up with the life of Jesus Christ, then you can pretty much chuck it.

Look at what Paul said about Jesus:

*"He is the image of the invisible God, the firstborn of all creation; **16** for in him all things in heaven and on earth were created, things visible and invisible, whether thrones or dominions or rulers or powers — all things have been created through him and for him. **17** He himself is before all things, and in him all things hold together." Colossians 1:15-17 (NRSV)*

Jesus is the exact representation of the Father. He is God, perfectly manifest in the flesh. In the Person of Christ, we find our perfect reference for who God the Father always has been and always will be. God, being perfectly holy and pure, came in the form of Jesus and got down in the dirt with the worst of us showing us what holiness actually looks like.

Holiness never has and never will have anything to do with living in a way that is separate from others. Holiness has its greatest expression in living a life of perfect love and enjoyment of those around us, warts and all.

The Holiness of God **actually manifests in His nearness to us and His love for us.**

If that were not the case, the Pharisees *(separatists)* would have been the most God-like people on the planet when Christ came. But we know that wasn't the case (see Matthew 23).

Think about it…

Before Jesus came, *supposedly*, mankind was evil, sinful, and unclean — *unable to connect with God*. But when Christ came, He had absolutely no problem hanging out and **connecting with** these *evil* and *dirty* people. Before anyone had prayed the *sinner's prayer*, or *repented*, Jesus came and He was not disgusted by us.

Instead, He loved and enjoyed people and brought out the best in them.

Christ coming in the form of humanity was God's message to us that He has always been and will forever be connected to us. God didn't take a downgrade when He became human. Instead He took the form He loved deeply and was happy to be forever married to. God found His best expression in the form of man — in Jesus Christ.

I know what you are thinking, *"But, Blaise, the Bible says that* **'sin separates us from God'** *so why are you saying that it doesn't?"*

We have to interpret the types and shadows of the Old Covenant through the Substance of the New Covenant. If you are viewing Christ through the lens of the Prophets, then you have it backwards. We must interpret the Prophets through the lens of Christ.

Look what Paul said to the Colossian church about trying to live through the shadows of the Old Covenant:

"Therefore do not let anyone judge you by what you eat or drink, or with regard to a religious festival, a New Moon celebration or a Sabbath day. 17 These are a shadow of the things that were to come; the reality, however, is found in Christ." Colossians 2:16-17 (NASB)

Paul tells these guys to stop worrying about Old Covenant rules and regulations about dietary laws, festival dates, and holy days.

He goes on to say that *these things* (Old Covenant laws and regulations) were *shadows* of the things that were to come. The writer of Hebrews expresses this same idea:

*"The law is only a **shadow** of the good things that are coming — not the realities themselves." Hebrews 10:1a (NASB)*

What do you think of when you see a shadow of a person going by you?

"I wonder who that is? I wonder how close they are?"

We don't observe the shadow intricately to figure out who the person is. We see the shadow and look up to see the person! Anytime you see a shadow, you start looking for its source. The shadow itself has no substance, but it serves to lead you to the object of its origin — the thing that carries reality.

*You embrace the **person**, not their **shadow**.*

The entire Old Covenant is to be seen exactly that way. The Prophets of the Old Covenant had revelation by the Spirit of God of things to come and of God's will concerning certain events and people, but they didn't have complete understanding of Him.

They experienced the character and nature of God, but only as in a shadow.

It was not until Christ came that the Substance of that shadow appeared in full view.

When He came, there was no need to go further into the shadows unless it was only to remind us why the Substance is really in front of us — and maybe to laugh at our earlier conclusions of what we thought the *Substance* might actually look like ☺

So what does this mean for us today?

And why are we talking about it?

We must remember: If there is an Old Covenant passage saying something about God we don't see to be true in the Person of Jesus Christ then we have to re-approach that verse in light of Jesus Christ.

Don't cough up your decaf too quickly.

I didn't say the passage isn't true or that it's wrong; I simply said that we *must* re-approach our conclusions about what that passage is actually trying to communicate *in **light** of **our current conclusion about Christ**.*

Let's look at what Paul, an avid student of the Old Covenant, had to say about the glory of New Covenant realities:

"[He] made us adequate as servants of a new covenant, not of the letter but of the Spirit; for the letter kills, but the Spirit gives life. 7 But if the ministry of death, in letters engraved on stones, came with glory, so that the sons of Israel could not look intently at the face of Moses because of the glory of his face, fading as it was, 8 how will the ministry of the Spirit fail to be even more with glory? 9 For if the ministry of condemnation has glory, much more does the ministry of righteousness abound in glory. 10 For indeed what had glory, in this case has no glory because of the glory that surpasses it." 2 Corinthians 3:6-9 (NASB)

The covenant given by Moses carried with it signs, wonders, and miracles. The parting of the Red Sea, the plagues of Egypt, the manna from heaven, and all of the other supernatural activity involved were still considered small in light of what has been given to us in Christ Jesus.

Even Moses and his glow-worm trick couldn't outdo the strobe light of what we have in the New Covenant. Literally, Paul said that the Old Covenant, in comparison to the New, had *no glory*.

Take it from Paul himself. He experienced both and he was an expert in the Old. After seeing the *mystery revealed,* he had nothing more to say about the mysterious shadow except that it was a *shadow* and had no *substance* in and of itself.

Approaching the Old Covenant with this in mind will be very helpful when we come across verses that seem to contradict what we know to be true about Jesus Christ.

Back to our original topic...

When the bible says that *sin separates us from God,* we have to look at it in light of the Person and work of Christ and in light of what we know to be true about the New Covenant. Let's take a look at this...

"But your iniquities have made a separation between you and your God, And your sins have hidden His face from you so that He does not hear." Isaiah 59:2 (NASB)

So do our sins really sever us from God? Do our sins cause God to be far from us and unable to hear our prayers? What does the New Covenant have to say about this situation?

"And although you were formerly alienated and hostile in mind, engaged in evil deeds, **22** *yet He has now reconciled you in His fleshly body through death..."* Colossians 1:21-22a (NASB)

The word *alienated* in the original language means *"to be shut out from one's fellowship and intimacy."* God didn't shut us out from fellowship with Him. We shut ourselves out. Sure, he closed the doors of Eden, but fellowship wasn't found in Eden. Fellowship was found in our hearts. That's why we still see men like Enoch and Abraham continuing to find fellowship with God after *the fall.*

Adam's sin didn't alienate God from Adam; it alienated Adam from God. Paul says in Colossians 1:21 that we became enemies of God **in our minds.** God was never our enemy; but we sure *thought*

115

He was.

When Adam and Eve sinned, instead of running to God, they ran and tried to hide *from God.*

Why?

Because they felt ashamed and had no idea what His reaction might be. They immediately became *"enemies* in their *minds* engaged in evil deeds."* The lie we believe that causes us to engage in sin is the same lie perpetuated after we engage in that behavior.

*"God is **not a good father** and hasn't provided what you need. He's not really fully on your side. You should go ahead and lie, cheat, steal, fornicate, play DDR, etc. to fulfill that need."*

Once you go through with the action, then there is nothing left to do but go deeper into hiding from God, because if He wasn't mad at you before, then He's definitely mad at you now. If He wasn't your enemy before, then He definitely is now. This is the kind of thinking that keeps people living in their sin cycles.

All the while, God is for us, loves us, and longs for us to come out from our hiding and embrace His forgiveness that has been available the whole time.

Does sin separate us from God? Does it cause Him to turn His back in distain? Does it make Him run for fear of getting *stained* by our mistakes? I would like you to look at yourself in the mirror and give an emphatic "HELL NO!"

In light of the reality of God expressed in and through Christ, we see that sin didn't actually separate us from God, but it made God come closer! Not that we should *"sin so that grace might abound"* (*see Romans 6:1-2),* but the revelation of His nearness is what actually brings life transformation!

God wants us to come to Him when we struggle or fail. He is completely unmoved and unhindered by our sin. In fact, He doesn't relate to us based upon our sin any longer. He relates to us based upon His gift of righteousness.

"He made Him who knew no sin to be sin on our behalf, so that we might become the righteousness of God in Him." 2 Corinthians 5:21 (NASB)

Jesus Christ completely became our sin when He was on the cross. When He became our sin, He was no less God than God the Father was. God never abandoned Jesus, because God cannot abandon Himself. You are just as righteous as Jesus, and God will never abandon you.

LOVE ISN'T A VERB AND SIN ISN'T EITHER (MOSTLY)

Remember that old *DC Talk* song, *Love is a Verb?*

(If not, you might be better for it).

Well, actually love is much more than a verb; love is a Person and His name is God.

We make the same mistake when we talk about sin. We suppose that sin is mostly about the actions we do or don't do. But sin is a *thing* to be dealt with, not an action to be changed.

Sin, in essence, is the darkened understanding produced through unbelief in God's goodness. Thankfully, Jesus dealt with this on the cross.

The Bible doesn't say that Jesus *committed sin* on our behalf, but that He *became sin*. You can't become an action, but you become a *thing*. And this *thing* called sin was what Jesus *became* in order to completely *destroy* it.

Hollywood seems to be full of stories like this. The lead character finds a way to die the death of the rest in order to save them. I think they're more inspired by *Holy Spirit* than the church would be comfortable admitting.

Recently I watched a *zombie movie*. Honestly, I'm not much of a *zombie guy,* but the movie was cool. Basically, the lead role finds a way to inject himself with a deadly sickness in order to become immune to the *Zombies* and help destroy them.

The Sci-Fi movie I recently watched was similar. The lead character *downloads* a computer virus into his brain so he can upload it to the mainframe computer of a brand new world. But in doing so, he will have to die in the process of uploading the new program to the new world. But he goes through with it for the good and the freedom of humanity.

Both of these are imperfect analogies, but they at least give us a natural example to help us understand these spiritual things.

Sin was not the action of Adam and Eve, but it was the unbelief that was allowed into their hearts that produced mistrust in God and ultimately a lack of friendship. The action was a manifestation of a sinful mindset which said, "God is not our friend." God's desire was friendship, but it couldn't happen with this fallen state of mind. So the Father become one of us and took on the sin of the world—the fallen state of mankind—the Adam-ic nature—*and had it completely destroyed on the cross.*

Sin is an identity; a location; a state of being.

Look at some of these Scriptures below that talk about the identity of someone who is still living in the state of unbelief:

"...for you were formerly darkness, but now you are Light in the Lord; walk as children of Light..." Ephesians 5:8 (NASB)

Paul doesn't say that you once *did darkness* but that you once *were darkness*.

*"For He rescued us from the domain **of darkness**, and transferred us to the **kingdom of** His beloved Son." Colossians 1:13 (NASB)*

In this passage Paul describes darkness not as *deeds* or *identity*, but as a *location*.

You once were *there* but now you are *here*. You once were *that* but now you are *this*.

Deeds spring from identity.

When you know your true identity as Light, then you will find yourself effortlessly manifesting the deeds of light. When you begin to see the new *location* you have been brought into, then you will start enjoying the heavenly realities all around you.

A WHOLE NEW PERSON IN A WHOLE NEW WORLD

I get so giddy just writing that subtitle above... I can hardly handle thinking about this reality because when I'm completely honest about it, *it just seems too good to be true.*

Let's look at this Scripture from the Apostle Paul in a number of different translations:

"Therefore if anyone is in Christ, he is a new creature; the old things passed away; behold, new things have come." 2 Corinthians 5:17 (NASB)

"For if a man is in Christ he becomes a new person altogether – the past is finished and gone, everything has become fresh and new." 2 Corinthians 5:17 (J.B Phillips)

"Therefore if any man is in Christ, he is a new creature; his old life has

disappeared, everything has become new about him." *2 Corinthians 5:17 (Knox Translation)*

"So if any man is in Christ he is in a new world, old things are passed away; behold, all things are become new." *2 Corinthians 5:17 (BAS)*

"When anyone is united to Christ, there is a new world – the old order has gone, and a new order has already begun." *2 Corinthians 5:17 (NEB)*

When anyone is awakened to their inclusion in the work of Christ, they begin to see with a whole different lens. I love the BAS translation of this verse that says *we are in a new world.* And then, of course, the J.B. Phillips states that *everything has become new about us.*

Have you ever been in a crowded room and felt like you were all alone? Have you ever been outside on a sunny day, but on the inside you felt horrible? When that happens it seems that the day might as well have been rainy and gloomy!

This is the experience of all those who are in bondage to the power of *lies* and *unbelief.*

Though the earth has been embraced by God's love and His redemption power, the majority of what these people see is colorless and grey. Of course, not everything is horrible. God shines His goodness on everyone regardless of belief or actions (Matthew 5:45), so everyone experiences His goodness one way or another. But the full experience of *life and life abundantly* only comes through the foundational understanding of His embrace and His love for us.

When we are awakened to His love and His goodness through faith in Jesus, it's like putting on brand new lenses.

Life turns Technicolor.

We start seeing that God has always been near us and for us. We transition from a kingdom of darkness and into a kingdom full of light! Adam's decision to *trust the deceiver* and break God's command, instead of trusting in God and obeying Him, is what we often call **the fall**.

What did he **fall** from? And what were the cosmic implications of this fall? Adam's fall didn't just affect him. It affected all of humanity.

"Therefore, just as through one man sin entered into the world, and death through sin, and so death spread to all men, because all sinned— **13** *for until the Law sin was in the world, but sin is not imputed when there is no law.* **14** *Nevertheless death reigned from Adam until Moses, even over those who had not sinned in the likeness of the offense of Adam, who is a type of Him who was to come." Romans 5:12-14 (NASB)*

That was a big chunk. Let me simplify it a bit with the Message Translation:

"You know the story of how Adam landed us in the dilemma we're in — first sin, then death, and no one exempt from either sin or death. That sin disturbed relations with God in everything and everyone, but the extent of the disturbance was not clear until God spelled it out in detail to Moses. So death, this huge abyss separating us from God, dominated the landscape from Adam to Moses. Even those who didn't sin precisely as Adam did by disobeying a specific command of God still had to experience this termination of life, this separation from God. But Adam, who got us into this, also points ahead to the One who will get us out of it." Romans 5:12-14

Adam's sin and his unbelief affected the entire human race who had yet to be born. There was absolutely no one who was exempt from this because everyone who was to be born from that time on would be born through the lineage of the first man, Adam.

Adam's sin was not just something that affected him. Just as Esau traded his *position* in the family for that fleeting meal, so Adam, on behalf of humanity, traded his rightful position of ruling and reigning over the earth for a fleeting meal.

Esau's mistake affected his entire lineage just as Adam's sin affected his *entire lineage*. (Thankfully, Christ redeemed Esau and His lineage).

Adam, along with all of humanity yet to be born in Adam, was seated in the place of authority. He didn't ascend to that place by effort, but rather was created for it and placed there by God.

When Adam made the transaction with the *deceiver,* he traded his rightful position of authority over the earth. Satan, the deceiver, then became what Paul calls *the god of this age (see 2 Corinthians 4:4).*

Of course, Satan never *rightfully* owned the earth, so really, he never *actually* owned the earth. He took a seat that Adam, along with all humanity, had vacated. The **fall** took us from the seat of authority and caused us to start seeing through the darkened lens of unbelief.

When the boss starts acting funny, the entire corporation gets weird.

That's what happened down here on good ole' earth. Mankind took a backseat and the entire vehicle started swerving.

Thankfully… that was not the end of the story.

The power of Jesus' death and resurrection cannot be overstated when it comes to understanding our redeemed identity and the restoration of our original position as humanity.

What was lost in Adam was restored in Christ.

"But the free gift is not like the transgression. For if by the transgression of the one the many died, much more did the grace of God and the gift by the grace of the one Man, Jesus Christ, abound to the many." Romans 5:15 (NASB)

"So then as through one transgression there resulted condemnation to all men, even so through one act of righteousness there resulted justification of life to all men. 19 For as through the one man's disobedience the many were made sinners, even so through the obedience of the One the many will be made righteous." Romans 5:18-19 (NASB)

Before the foundation of the earth God chose us, in Christ, to be holy, perfect, and blameless (Ephesians 1:4). It was His good intention and His good purpose to have humanity as a gem that would never lose her value. And though she **fell,** she never lost her original worth.

Through the incarnation, God shouted to the human race, *"You are worth it! You always have been and always will be! You are worth GOD."*

You don't pay trash for treasure. The value of the purchased object is equal to the value of the exchanged currency.

Do you understand what this means? God showed us our value by laying down His life for us all. This was our value — **GOD.** You are worth more than you could ever imagine.

OUR RESTORED POSITION

In Adam, humanity lost its position as rulers of the earth and came under the dominion of darkness. But in Christ, we have been fully redeemed and restored to our original position.

*4 But God, being rich in mercy, because of His great love with which He loved us, 5 even **when we were dead** in our transgressions, **made us*** *alive* together with Christ *(by grace you have been saved),* **6** *and* __raised__ __us up with Him__*, and* __seated us with Him in the heavenly places__ *in Christ Jesus,* **7** *so that in the ages to come He might show the surpassing riches of His grace in kindness toward us in Christ Jesus."* Ephesians 2:4-7

When Christ died and rose from the dead, He took us with Him. Jesus Christ is forever the vicarious man (the substitute) for all mankind. With all the talk about the *elect* and the *chosen*, we often forget to talk about the One who we know is actually chosen and elect—Jesus Christ.

He is the One Man who did what no man could do. He kept our side of the bargain in relationship with the Father and put us back in good standing with God.

Adam dropped us low, but Jesus raised us higher.

WE ALL KNOW WHAT LOVE LOOKS LIKE

When Jesus came to the world, He didn't come with small vision or limited expectations. Jesus' coming to earth had universal implications because He is the God who loves the *entire world*.

We have to start with God's heart and His original intention. God's heart has always been and always will be full redemption and the embrace of every person that He has created. God didn't dream up humanity with the intention of destroying some and saving others.

His one and only intention has been to love and embrace every single unique individual on the planet.

I have run into folks over the years who seem to carry a strong sense that God **created some people** for friendship with Him and others for the purpose of eternal destruction. *"Somehow,"* they would say, *"in God's infinite wisdom, this is justice and love."*

That kind of talk makes me scratch my head and go, *"Huh...really?"*

When we start talking about God like He is so beyond our understanding, it gives us an excuse to come up with all kinds of ideas about Him and confirm them through a simple, *"Well, His ways are higher than our ways..."* type of statement.

One problem with this type of statement is that it is a bible verse being quoted completely out of context in order to prove the opposite point from which is was originally written.

The fact is the very context of Isaiah's prophecy regarding God's ways being higher than our ways actually begins with a plea from the heart of God for mankind to *change our thinking* and come up to His level! It's almost as though He is saying, *"Your thoughts are way too small! You need to think on my level. Come up here and think like I think, and you'll start acting like I act!"*

Check it out:

*"Let the wicked forsake his way And the unrighteous man **his thoughts**; And let him return to the Lord, And He will have compassion on him, And to our God, For He will abundantly pardon.8 "For **My thoughts are not your thoughts**, Nor are your ways My ways," declares the Lord.9 "For as the heavens are higher than the earth, So are My ways **higher** than your ways And **My thoughts than your thoughts.**" Isaiah 55:7-9*

The other problem with the *"God's ways are beyond us"* rationale is that it goes directly against what Christ revealed to us. We have to make the shift from this *Far Away God* mindset to the New Covenant reality of the God who has revealed Himself completely in Jesus Christ as *Emmanuel, God with Us.*

Remember what Jesus said to Phillip when he was stuck in the *unknowable God* idea?

"He who has seen Me has seen the Father; how can you say, 'Show us the Father'?" John 14:8 (NASB)

And remember what the writer of Hebrews said about the way we used to see God versus what Christ has now revealed?

*"God, after He spoke long ago to the fathers in the prophets in many portions and in many ways, 2 in these last days **has spoken to us in His Son**, whom He appointed heir of all things, through whom also He made the world. 3 And He is the radiance of His glory and **the exact representation of His nature**, and upholds all things by the word of His power." Hebrews 1:1-3a (NASB)*

Jesus *is God.* We are not waiting for a new manifestation of God or a secret side of His personality to be revealed. All that He is in His character and nature has been made clear in the life and Person of Jesus Christ.

I think this revelation is central to understanding our Papa. I have heard people say that God creating some for damnation is somehow *love* due to the *unknowablity* of God and His ways.

But when we start to filter doctrines and ideas like this through the revealed Person of Christ, we find that they get barfed up by the Son of God because of their lukewarm mixture.

If Jesus is God and God is love, then we have a clear definition of love.

Love is not an *abstract mystery*. God is love.

And God has been revealed in the Person of Jesus Christ.

Some of the best theology I have ever heard has come from random "secular" (whatever that means) artists. I especially appreciate the theology expressed in the movie I mentioned earlier called *Forrest Gump:*

"Jenny, I'm not a smart man, but I know what love is." ~Forrest Gump

It's not rocket science, and it doesn't take a PhD to know what love looks like. Even the unbeliever knows what love is... In fact, it's pretty simple:

"Greater **love** *has* **no** *one than this, that one lay down his life for his friends." ~Jesus (see John 15:3)*

Paul looked at what Jesus did and went one step further, saying not only did He do this for His *friends* but while we were still *"His enemies"* Christ died for us (Romans 5:8).

He didn't only die for the *few* who could pull themselves up by their bootstraps of *faith* and *goodness.* But instead, He died for all while all were still His enemies, opening the doorway for the narrow road to turn into the broad place. He showed us in His life and death how He felt about the most unfaithful of us all.

In His incarnation He shouted a hearty *"I LOVE YOU"* to the religiously faithful and the religiously murderous—counting us all equal benefactors of His mercy.

Jesus had no prerequisite for giving His life, and He still has no prerequisites for those who would come to Him, except that they actually do just that—*come.* And stepping out and coming to Him is the very simple *act* of trust that He *requires.* Just come.

Again, great theology from the so-called *secular world:*

"Come as you are..." –Kurt Cobain of Nirvana

THE HAPPY GOSPEL

Recently I was sitting around a campfire with some of my buddies when I got in a conversation with two girls from Belgium. They were spending a few days in Nashville while they were in the U.S. and staying with some friends of mine.

As I listened to different conversations around the campfire, I heard one of the girls say,

"I don't want to talk about this anymore."

I saw her start shutting down because there was a lot of talk about God, so I immediately jumped into the conversation,

"Hey…so what do you do?" I asked genuinely, *"like, what's your job?"*

She began to tell me about how she was inventing a new ventilation system within hospital surgery rooms. She is also getting her PhD.

I was seriously blown away. *"We are in the presence of greatness and we didn't know it!"* I said with excitement. She was a bit embarrassed but appreciated the compliment.

I proceeded to tell her how amazing and creative she was, and I could tell that she was a little taken back by my statements. I decided that instead of trying to convince her to *"be a Christian like me,"* I just decided to be a Christian and love the hell out of her.

Then I turned to her friend who was a little more open to the *God-conversation* and asked, *"Can I tell you something amazing about God?"*

She smiled and then obliged.

I was absolutely jacked up on the joy of Jesus at the moment, so she was very intrigued, to say the least.

"God is the most joyful being in existence," I said with a big-ole smile plastered on my face.

"Oh really?" she said with a grin.

"Who is the happiest person you have ever met?" I asked.

Then she proceeded to tell me all about her mother and how kind and happy she is. I loved watching her face light up as she told this story. I began to tell her that the happiness and kindness of her mother, as great as she is, is only a slight picture of the vastness of God's personality and character.

"That makes sense..." she said curiously.

I continued to tell her that I saw Jesus in her. I told her Jesus was there all the time whether she knew it or not, believed it or not, or even cared.

Then she told me she was an atheist.

"Awesome," I said with a strange sincerity.

(My response even surprised me.)

This *weirded* her out even more. Mind you, I was so hammered on Holy Spirit that night, and as soon as I pulled up to the house where everyone was hanging out, I immediately felt the joy of Jesus in my being, and I just rode that wave all the way in.

When an atheist sees a genuinely happy Christian who doesn't talk about hell and judgment and actually feels free to be *normal*, I find it usually throws them off a bit.

She was thrown off...

"Well, I guess I believe in faith... yeah, that's what I believe in," she

said.

"Wow…amazing! Me too!" I said joyfully.

"Everyone knows there's something… Someone out there — or right here — we talk to when we need help. Ya know, like, 'Hey, I could use some help right now…hook me up, whoever you are.'"

She giggled. She knew she was caught…. *"I do that!"* she said.

"Yeah, I know you do!" I said. *"It really doesn't matter so much what you believe about God. The fact is, He believes in you. He loves you whether you know it or not, feel it or not, or whether you love Him back. God loves you so much!"*

I saw it in her eyes. It was starting to click.

"Yeah, I believe that…" was her confession.

I was so drunk on the presence of Jesus by the time she said that.

I felt so much glory around that campfire, and I could see the happiness of Jesus on her face as she was discovering that there was Someone bigger who actually *cared for her and loved her.*

Before we left, I looked at her and said, *"Try this out next time you talk to that Someone… just call Him **Jesus.**"*

She smiled and said, *"Okay, I'll do that."*

Somehow, without warning her of God's *judgment*, telling her how bad she was, or demanding that she repent of her wickedness, this young Atheist became a believer in the God and Father of Jesus Christ — the One who created her and loves her unconditionally.

So much of the evangelistic ministry these days is based on making people afraid of *what God might do to them* if they don't *come to Him* and *get right with Him*. Does anyone else see a problem with this kind of thinking?

"Hey guys, God loves you, but if you don't get your act together, then He's going to torture you forever."

Or,

*"God is really mad at you because you are a sinner. But if you repent today and become a Christian, **then** God will love you."*

Let me get this straight, God hates me until I believe in Him. But once I believe in Him, then He'll start to love me. So, my right *believing* makes God love me? And my *wrong believing* makes God hate me?

I think this meme I found online says it better than I can:

Don't get me wrong. I understand that God is a *judge*. But judgment has been given to the Son... and guess what? He didn't come to judge, but to save.

Check out this quote by a theologian, Robert F. Capon:

"This Son, strangely, does not judge, but rather saves. Not only in this verse (John 12:47), therefore, but throughout the Gospel of John, there lurks the image of the rigged trial, of a judgment at which the judge is

shamelessly in cahoots with the guilty world and utterly determined to acquit it no matter what." -Robert Capon[4]

I think we get really confused when we begin to interpret Jesus Christ through Old Testament stories and even New Testament verses instead of interpreting the entire Bible through the Person of Jesus. In His life and ministry He revealed God perfectly, so we mustn't pit Scriptures of judgment against the life and words of Jesus Himself.

"He who believes in Him is not judged; he who does not believe has been judged already, because he has not believed in the name of the only begotten Son of God." John 3:18 NASB

The word *judge* in this passage is the word *krinō (in Greek)* which has multiple meanings, all of which are not negative.

1. to separate, put asunder, to pick out, select, choose

2. to approve, esteem, to prefer

3. to determine, resolve, decree

4. to pronounce an opinion concerning right and wrong[5]

So we can't just automatically think that it is negative towards people in every situation.

But really, at the end of the day, Jesus is not judging anyone, according to this passage at least. In fact, He says that anyone who doesn't believe what He said about Himself is already *judged, living in darkness, alienated in their hearts and minds from the life of God* because of their unbelief. That **does not** mean that **He judges or condemns them** in a negative way.

---

[4] Robert Capon, Kingdom, Grace, Judgment (Grand Rapids: W.m. B. Eerdmans Publishing Co, 1989): 367.
[5] Definitions taken from www.blueletterbible.org

And don't forget Paul's declaration in Acts 17 that God *has judged* mankind in righteousness through the act of Jesus Christ's death and resurrection.

The fact is, all of humanity fell in Adam and became darkened in understanding. We lost revelation of the goodness of God and began to make *gods* after our own image instead of realizing we were in His image. We became like children who ran from their Father. When He came in the Person of Jesus, He didn't come to **judge** or to **condemn**.

Instead, He came to seek and save all who were lost. And who was lost? It was not only one or a few of the *bad kids* in Humanity's High School; no, it was every last one of us from the *Valedictorian* to the *dropouts*.

"Here is a trustworthy saying that deserves full acceptance: Christ Jesus came into the world to save sinners--of whom I am the worst." 1 Timothy 1:15 (NIV)

Paul, of course, the former-religiously-motivated-murderer, thought of himself as the worst of the worst sinners. But I guarantee you this, we are all in the same boat, and we all fell from the highest height to the lowest low and became the worst of the worst along with Adam, Cain, Saul of Tarsus, bugs bunny, and the rest of the gang. And I'm thankful for that fact because it only takes *our simple unbelief* to take us low just as it only takes the *simple faithfulness of Jesus* and our trust in Him to turn the tables...

Let's look at a few more Scriptures that declare the all-inclusive work of Jesus:

"He is the atoning sacrifice for our sins, and not only for ours but also for the sins of the whole world." 1 John 2:2 (NIV)

John declares that Jesus's sacrifice didn't only atone for the sins of believers (*"our sins"*), but it did the job for the sins of the entire world.

"For it is for this we labor and strive, because we have fixed our hope on the living God, who is the Savior of all men, especially of believers." 1 Timothy 4:10 (NASB)

Paul says to Timothy that God is the *Savior of all mankind*. In order for Him to be the Savior of all, He actually has to save all. Otherwise, He would have been called the *Savior of some men*.

I am **not** a universalist. But I am an honest reader who has decided not to cut out the Scriptures that declare a universal atonement. And I do carry the same desire that is in God's very own heart—for all to come to the knowledge of the truth. I also have a strong hope for that desire to be fulfilled. The hope is not based on sentiment—even though love involves sentiment—but, it's based on God's *desire* and God's *ability* to save (see 2 Peter 3:9 and Job 42:2).

We must approach Scripture in its entirety and be open to the fact that Christ's cross might have been more powerful than we realized and God's desire might actually be possible (see 2 Peter 3:9).

This, my friends, is good news!

I love what the Apostle Paul has to say to the accusation that Jesus is still in the condemning business:

"Who then is the one who condemns? No one. Christ Jesus who died-- more than that, who was raised to life--is at the right hand of God and is also interceding for us." Romans 8:33-34 (NIV)

So, according to the revelation of the Apostle Paul, Jesus is standing beside the Father as the *forever-go-between* of God and man—not because God wants to kill man, but as an advocate for Man to come to God with confidence and joy; reassured of our rightful place in the kingdom.

Condemnation never has and never will come from Jesus Christ.

If anyone at anytime experiences condemnation, they can be sure that it is of their own choice and unbelief in God's goodness.

The way to the *no-condemnation-life* has already been opened for all to come and set up camp forever in the presence of ever-lasting love and acceptance. Now, through Christ, God has embraced and accepted the entirety of disobedient mankind and pulled them to Himself. What is there left to do but turn from the illusion of separation, and simply embrace the One who has already embraced us?

CHAPTER 7
QUESTIONS AND CONCLUSIONS
Asking good questions and finding the good God

Conclusion. Closure. Destination. Arrival.

ANSWERS.

We all appreciate a good *"The End"* after paying $15.00 for a 3D movie. Even if there is a *"to be continued..."* we eventually get tired of continuous sequels.

That's why *most* sequels fail. With the exception of the *Back to the Future* and *Star Wars* trilogies... and probably others...

Anyways...

Back to my point.

We all want an **answer** to the hard questions about God, faith, and the seemingly unknown. It's often seen as a weakness to say, *"I don't know."*

Especially in the West.

But I have been ever-so-challenged to keep my conclusions loose and the conversation open when it comes to topics such as these.

I once heard about a person who had a *vision* in which he was floating in outer space. Suddenly, he saw a huge meteor flying towards him at mock speed. He opened his arms to catch the flaming rock when suddenly he awoke from the vision. He distinctly heard the Holy Spirit speak to Him saying,

"This is what it's like to try to fit me into man's theology."

Wow. Whether or not this guy actually *heard God* or not is debatable. But, sheesh, that analogy sure does explain it pretty well, doesn't it?

Humility is the mark of maturity.

Unteachability is the mark of stupidity.

I have concluded that I must remain open to *change* because I will *always be learning*. In fact, change is the very heart of true repentance. The more I learn, the more I repent. And that repentance is always a *joyful repentance* since truth only leads me to the *goodness* of the *good news*.

I love this quote by John Crowder,

"If there is any area you consider yourself to be in a better mood than God, you may want to re-evaluate that area of your theology." –John Crowder (Cosmos Reborn)

When I find an angry God in what is popularly called *sound doctrine*, I immediately question this conclusion based upon what I know of God in Christ Jesus. I don't claim to have all of the answers to everyone's questions, but I am content to *know nothing* and find my conclusions in the Work and Person of Christ Jesus.

"For I resolved to know nothing while I was with you except Jesus Christ and him crucified." 1 Corinthians 2:2 (NIV)

ASKING GOOD QUESTIONS

Once I began to understand the *grace of God* and the truth of His nature shown in the life and Person of Jesus, I started to ask questions about what I had always been told and always believed about the gospel and our motivation for preaching it.

Does God love everyone?

Is God the Father of all humanity?

Did God really leave it up to us to save ourselves?

*Do **good** Dads scare their kids into obedience?*

Is it really <u>obedience</u> that God is after?

Who really killed Michael Jackson?

It's questions like these that helped me dive deeper into my journey of grace. The answers to these kinds of questions reveal what we truly believe about the core character of God. And what we believe about His character will directly influence the way we relate to Him and to others.

If *fear* is really the motivation for bringing people to God, then we should be walking around shouting about God's anger and wrath. And that, in fact, is what many people do. And if we take this idea one step further, then couldn't we easily come to conclusions like this?

God is very angry at the sinners of the world until they turn to Him in repentance. In order to be godly (like God), then I also need to be angry at sinners until they believe what I am preaching and turn to be saved.

I hate to say it, but the conclusion of this kind of thinking always ends up in exclusion and hate.

"But Blaise, doesn't the Bible say that God hates His enemies?"

Sure. The Bible says a lot of things. That's one reason why we actually have to *rightly divide the word of truth (2 Timothy 2:15).*

Just because *the bible says* something doesn't mean that **God** is actually saying that *thing*. Relax... let me explain...

Paul, in essence, says to Timothy, *"Dude, make sure you handle the Law and the Prophets' writings accurately – in light of the finished work of Christ. Otherwise, you're gonna really have some jacked up theology and a wrong view of who God is." (see 2 Timothy 2:15)*

When we interpret Christ through the prophets, we usually end up confused or thinking that Jesus didn't fully reveal the Father when He came. But when we interpret the prophets through the revelation of Jesus, then we can begin to come to proper conclusions about our Papa.

So, Blaise, are you saying that the Prophets and teachers of the Law didn't say everything perfectly?

Well, honestly, yes. They didn't see or say everything perfectly. Sure, they said many of "God's words," but they really didn't see correctly or have a clue what they were saying the majority of the time. Oh, and by the way, they were still human—*fully human*— with all of the idiosyncrasies and emotional hiccups of being one of us.

Look what Peter said, post-cross-revelation, about the *Prophets*:

10 *As to this salvation, the prophets who prophesied of the grace that would come to you, made careful searches and inquiries,* **11** *seeking to know what person or time the Spirit of Christ within them was* *indicating as He predicted the sufferings of Christ and the glories to follow. 12 It was revealed to them that they were not serving themselves, but you, in these things which now have been announced to you through those who preached the gospel to you by the Holy Spirit sent from heaven – things into which angels long to look." 1 Peter 1:10-12 (NASB)*

If you'll allow me the *Blaise Foret Modern Version* license, then I'll share my thoughts on this passage ☺

"These Prophets who lived under the Old Covenant spent time under the influence of the Holy Spirit and spoke about the gospel that would soon be revealed fully. Once they were finished speaking, they ran home to study the transcriptions they just announced. Literally, these guys had no clue what they were talking about! But it wasn't them – it was Christ influencing them and speaking through them. As they studied, it was revealed to them that the time was coming when God would come to man and suffer for man, as man, and bring man into glory. Now, don't think they had a full grasp of this! It was still in types and shadows, but they knew there'd be a day when the mystery would be revealed, and they longed for that day! Even the angels themselves couldn't see this stuff with clarity... it was huge! It was massive! It is the very revelation of Christ, Emmanuel, God with Us and in Us forever! Absolutely unheard of in times past."

Now, if you still think I'm exaggerating the revelation (or lack thereof) of the Old Covenant Prophets and Law Preachers let me continue with more understanding from the New Covenant and from Christ Himself.

Jesus, during the famous *Sermon on the Mount* said of the law and of Moses, "You've heard it said in the Law of Moses _____, *but I say* _____." (See Matthew 5)

Who was it that inspired Moses to write the law?

Where did the Law come from?

140

If you answered, *"God"* then give yourself a pat on the back and a Jolly Rancher. You are correct.

If you answered, *"Jesus"* then add a smiley face sticker to the former prize.

Here is **God** in the Person of Jesus telling the folks,

"Guys, the Law of Moses tells you not to murder. ***But I tell you,*** *don't hate people or it's the same thing."*

So did God (Jesus) talk to Moses or not? Did God (Jesus) give Moses an accurate picture of Himself in the Law?

Obviously, the Law is full of *good things,* and it's perfect and holy. But even the Law, as perfect as it was, couldn't fully express the character and nature of God as perfectly as **Christ Himself** did. Otherwise, there would have been no need for Christ to come!

Jesus came and brought a whole new understanding of God.

"You guys think I want you to kill each other for doing bad things. But actually, that's only in there because you guys have such a hard time forgiving one another! I actually want to live in you and change you from the inside out so that you'll be as forgiving and as loving as Me."

Can you imagine the Pharisees thinking, *"This guy, Jesus, is here telling us that Moses missed it, and He has greater revelation than Moses? What a heretic!"*

It's not that Moses *missed it.* Moses just didn't have the full picture. In fact, ***no one had the full picture.*** Jesus and Jesus alone **was** the full picture, and when He came, everything became clear.

Interestingly enough, some folks still act like Jesus never came and still take their cues from Moses and the Prophets.

Calling down judgment and condemnation on unbelievers and sinners.

Living as though following rules and regulations will please God.

Finding their identity in struggling as "just a sinner saved by grace."

And many other faulty mindsets.

What do we know about these things in light of the Person of Jesus and the revelation of the gospel?

Calling down judgment? Jesus told the guys that they were of a demonic spirit when they wanted to call down *fire* on the unbelieving Samaritans (Luke 9:55). *Not sure what to do about this.* It seems like God did this to Sodom and Gomorrah pre-cross. Elisha also did this to those who came to capture him. But Jesus had something different to say about it. Food for thought...

Condemnation on the sinners? No way. Jesus actually broke the Law of Moses in order to fulfill the law of love. He told the woman caught in adultery to rise up and go live life abundantly — without the mar and the scar of the false identity called *sin* (John 8:11).

Living for rules and regulations? Following religious rules and rituals have zero bearing on whether or not God was pleased with us. Instead, Jesus calls for us to *die to our ability to please God* — finding ourselves wrapped up in a brand new identity, raised up and hidden in Christ (Matthew 19:21, Mark 10:21, Galatians 6:15, Colossians 3:1-3).

It seems like there is definitely a difference between the perception of God the writers of the Old Covenant had versus the God Jesus Christ had and revealed.

We find another example of a flawed human being prophesying judgment in the Old Testament when we look at Isaiah 1-5.

Isaiah shouts *"woe"* to just about everybody and everything under the sun.

Do you ever feel like this..? ...feeling the tension of God's holiness and mankind's disobedience?

As a believer it's easy to see only the negative and want to call down judgment on everyone! But just because we "feel the Spirit" stirring our hearts with revelation of God's holiness doesn't mean we need to turn and condemn a deceived and hurting world.

In fact, when Isaiah got to the throne room in chapter 6, we see a different declaration being spoken about the earth.

*"Holy, Holy, Holy is the Lord Almighty! The **whole earth is full of His glory**!" Isaiah 6:*

Really? The earth? Full of His glory?

It's all about the lens that you see through.

Do you see God's love and glory on **everyone** and **everything** *regardless of the circumstances?* Or do you see the circumstances and actions of people and allow those to dictate what you believe about them?

When we see trash, we will declare condemnation.

When we see glory, we will declare glory.

When we see treasure, we will declare its value.

Christ came to give us the perfect revelation of the Father. Those who had studied their "bibles" for years and knew the most about theology had no idea who Jesus was. Those who had *eyes to see and ears to hear* the voice of the kind Father recognized Jesus when He came.

The Bible is only beneficial because it reveals the Person of Christ.

Inasmuch as the Bible is used for this purpose, it will be valuable. But when used for other purposes, it can be damaging and dangerous.

I believe the best way to hold to the *66 canonized books of the Bible* is to do so only in light of the revealed Person of God through Jesus Christ. Otherwise, we'll use the bible for all kinds of religious funny business.

Seeing Christ as the central focus of the *Bible* and the main point of life allows us to change our perspective on humanity and see them *all included* in God's love *before they change*. We begin to see them as valuable and worthy apart from their actions. We *no longer* see people according to the flesh, but according to God's original intention, and we treat them accordingly (see 2 Corinthians 5:13-15).

I realize this raises all sorts of questions in the mind of the modern evangelical—questions about salvation, belief, and faith in the work of Christ.

Is faith necessary? Of course. What we believe about God's love for us changes the way we experience reality, whether it be through a darkened lens of unbelief or the perfectly clear lens of Christ's cross.

And, of course, how does this affect our eternity? Personally, I won't claim to know who is going where and when the opportunity for repentance (change of mind) ceases to be available to them. I don't think it's wise to make quick judgments about who's going to heaven and who's going to burn in hell.

Unfortunately, it seems that many Christians love their ideas of hell more than they love the individuals they claim are going there.

Obviously, *repentance (metanoia)* and faith in Christ's work are a major factor in the salvation experience, but *our faith and repentance* does not *create* our redemption. Christ washed away the sin of every individual — past, present, and future. And our *simple trust* in that reality brings us into the experience of this finished work.

I do not hold such a high view of *hell* and a low view of the *kindness, patience,* and *love* of God that I would claim to put **anyone**, at **anytime**, outside of the limits of God's kindness and love or His **desire** and **ability** to awaken them to repentance.

The bible is full of many passages claiming that people who don't repent and believe the gospel will be lost for all eternity. And it's full of passages that seem to imply there is opportunity for repentance and change of heart beyond the grave. Regardless, this does not change the way I preach the good news to people I come into contact with *today*. Our job is to preach the good news of God's love shown perfectly in the person of Jesus. No one is excluded from that love, and that love is what will awaken faith in the heart of those who have yet to believe.

I will leave the other stuff up to Jesus and let Him, in His perfect love, decide the fate of individuals *who refuse to accept His acceptance of them.*

At the end of the day, I don't expect that we'll mostly be surprised at His anger but rather mesmerized by the magnitude of His mercy. The scandal most likely won't be the revelation of His wrath but the absolute absence of what we call *fairness* and *justice* (see Matthew 20:15).

MOHAMMED HUGGED JESUS

Our view of God affects the way we treat humanity and the way we present the good news about God to them.

In October 2008 I had just moved to Kansas City, MO and decided to go out on an *evangelism outreach* to a haunted house. While I was there, I ended up talking to a couple dudes who were hanging out in the alleyway next to the house. One of them was a short Caucasian dude, and the other was a tall dark-skinned man from Ethiopia or somewhere in Northern Africa. As we spoke, the tall African man suddenly got in my face and violently said, "One question for you! Jesus or Mohammed?!?"

"Hmmm…" I thought, *"If I say Jesus, then he'll get pissed and either kick my butt or totally shut me out. If I say 'Mohammed' then I'd be lying…"*

So, I said, *"Jesus."*

Just like I thought. He got very angry.

He reared back to punch me…

"Well, this is it," I thought, *"the moment of 'persecution' for Jesus. Here we go…"*

He stopped and frustratingly said, *"If we were in prison right now, then I'd knock your head off…"*

"Man, I'm glad we're not in prison." I thought to myself.

And then something funny happened.

I just looked at him and suddenly began feeling so much love.

I just loved the dude—it was crazy. It made absolutely no sense whatsoever. I literally had no fear in that moment because *perfect love* had overtaken my being! I was drunk with love for this man!

I looked him in the eye and said, *"Mohammed, come on man, it's all good,"* as I stuck out my hand for a side-five/hand-shake, *"come on man… you're a good man; you're a good man, Mohammed, you're a good man."*

Really? Mohammed? The guy who was about to beat me up was a *good man?* Hmmm... someone needed a theological straightening out. This guy was an unbeliever and possibly a murderer. He was *not a good man.* But, that's not what I told him. Sure enough, I told him he was a *good man.* I found myself saying it from a deeper part of my heart that felt like an artesian well that couldn't be controlled. It's as though the Apostle Paul's description of his ministry to the world was being explained in me and through me at that moment. Look what Paul said:

*"For Christ's love compels us, because **we are convinced that one died for all, and therefore all died.** 15 And he died for all, that those who live should no longer live for themselves but for him who died for them and was raised again. 16 **So from now on we regard no one from a worldly point of view.** Though we once regarded Christ in this way, we do so no longer. 17 Therefore, if anyone is in Christ, the new creation has come: The old has gone, the new is here!" 2 Corinthians 5:14-17 (NIV)*

Without even knowing it, **I began to see this man as *good* and as the *new creation* Jesus had always intended him to be.** That's why my heart bubbled up with love and told him the truth about his identity in the Father's eyes.

He was named after the prophet of Islam, but God had a different identity for him.

He had been taught to hate and to bring violence on those who thought differently than he did, but God had a completely different intention for him. God saw this young man according to how He created him and what He created him for.

God saw this man according to the finished work of Christ for all humanity. God saw this man's sins as atoned for and forgiven.

God saw this man as someone included in His love who was yet to be told!

Mohammed melted. Right there. Right into my arms.

He slapped the hand-shake, pulled me close, and gave me a huge hug!

He told me about how he had been in prison. I told him God loved him and wanted him to know it. *He turned from a hardened man of violence to a soft-hearted man who was melted by love in that moment.*

Religion comes in and tells you God is angry at people until they *repent and believe*. It literally creates a large chasm between *GOD* and *unbelievers* that is **just... not... real**.

It also creates a gap between *believers* and *unbelievers* that was never intended to be there.

How many times have Christians *witnessed* to *unbelievers* in such a way that made them feel like a piece of trash that came from hell and was headed back to hell unless they *prayed a prayer* in that moment?

This is a more than regular occurrence.

The problem with this mindset is that it has absolutely nothing to do with the way Jesus Christ approached the world. He did not come to reveal how worthless mankind was; rather He came to reveal our original value found. He didn't come to tell us how bad we were but how worth it we were — worth enough for Him to lay down His life in exchange for ours.

The word *reconcile* in 2 Corinthians 5:19 has to do with exchanging two objects of equal value. Our life was literally worth His life. He has created us in His image and as His equal.

We are His brothers (Psalm 22:22)

We are His offspring (Acts 17)

We are His heirs (Romans 8:17)

We share His throne (Ephesians 3:6)

What if Christ's work really was able to undo Adam's mistake? What if Christ's act was really *"much more"* effective than *"the transgression"? (Romans 5:15)* What if what Christ did was not just enough to affect those who would muster up the ability to believe it, but literally the entire cosmos? (see 2 Corinthians 5:19)

The answer to these questions will affect the way we live our lives and the way we perceive the entire world and every human being we meet!

God's love doesn't have an expiration date. He loves everyone, and He sees us all as complete because of Christ. Even in the midst of our junk. We are all His, and we are complete because of His work. We have all been included in the universal atoning working of the cross and we no longer call anyone unholy or unclean (see Acts 10:15, 28). We share this truth in love in order to present every person *as complete in Christ (see Colossians 1:28).*

CHANGING OUR THOUGHTS ABOUT GOD: HE IS WITH US AND HE IS FOR US

The Apostle Paul declared of himself *pre-conversion* that *"it pleased God to reveal His Son **in me** that I might preach Him **in the nations**." (Galatians 1:16)*

The Greek word Paul used about himself and about the nations is the word *en*. This word has the same meaning for both Paul and for those he had yet to preach to. The truth is, God came to Paul and revealed Paul's original design and revealed that Christ had been in Him all along.

There was no reason to keep running from destiny or to remain blind to the truth. So Paul embraced the reality of Christ within and then declared that reality to the nations!

Christ is with you, in you, and all around you! He is *"not far from any of us"* was Paul's declaration to the Pagans in *Acts 17*. *"In Him we live and move and have our being!"* (Acts 17:28) This is our declaration to an unbelieving world waiting to hear the good news about a good God who is with them, in them, and loves them dearly.

Hearing this truth is what brings true change in the lives and hearts of people. That change is simply called "metanoia" in the Greek or "repentance" in English.

I know... I just said a dirty word.

Repent.

Some of you have been waiting for me to finally use the word. Others have been thankful that I haven't. Some will say I don't "preach repentance enough," while others might cringe if I do.

Personally, I believe that **repent** is a dirty word. I can't stand it.

But let me explain.

The word **repent** was not originally in the biblical text but was translated from the Greek word *metanoia*. Unfortunately, the word *repent* doesn't quite capture the essence of the original Greek word *metanoia* that was used by the authors of the New Testament. This word simply means to "change your mind" or "come to the knowledge of the truth."

I appreciate the way that Andre Rabe has explained this:

These early Christian leaders dealt with this problem by developing the concept of 'doing penance' or repentance, as a way to solve the problem of sin after conversion. It was meant to make forgiveness possible, but difficult, so that people would not take advantage of it.

This lead to a very complicated system of categorizing sin and an equally complicated process of repentance, involving the depth and sincerity of a person's feelings of regret, together with various 'acts of penance', as prescribed by a priest. These acts of penance in effect became one's own atonement for one's sins.

By the time the scriptures were translated into Latin, these doctrines, rather than the actual text, influenced the translation more. And so metanoia was translated as 'acts of penance' and later as repentance. Penance implies a payment.

This translation of metanoia has caused so much misunderstanding. In fact, the common understanding of the word repentance does not even occur in the original text! The word repentance still carries the same flavour as penance. Re-penance ... a repetition of penance.

In regards to the Latin Vulgate and its use of *repentance* Rabe says,

"...Often it was pointed out that the concepts of repentance and penance are not present in the Greek word metanous. Lorenzo Valla, a theologian, again pointed out this error in translation in 1430. However, because these concepts were so ingrained within the religious mindset, the corrections were overruled and the error of penance was retained.[6]

That will change the way that you see those signs held up on the street corner that say "REPENT!"

Often, the guys carrying those signs don't even know what they are saying or where the word itself comes from. When a word is not understood in its original context it can often be misused to

---

[6] https://ginomai.org/a/676

hurt or condemn people. That's exactly what has happened with the word *repent*.

Next time you hear a preacher tell you to repent, feel free to smile and say, "Gladly!" Repentance is not a drudgery. I joyfully *repent* every single day. I simply change my mind about the wrong thinking and begin to think true thoughts. Thoughts always produce actions. A true change of mind will bring about a change of life. So, change your thinking! Believe the truth!

What is the truth? The truth is that God has never been far from you! In fact, He has never been far from *anyone!*

He is waiting for humanity to wake up to their origin and open their eyes to the goodness of their Father. You come from God and your destination is God. He is your loving Father and though you may not currently recognize or believe that, it doesn't change that reality. He's longing for all of humanity to *remember* and *return* to Him.

The Psalmist declares in Psalm 22 that eventually the whole earth will awaken to their friendship with God. Check it out…

"All the ends of the earth will remember and turn to the LORD, and all the families of the nations will bow down before him." Psalm 22:27

In the heart of every man lies the knowledge of where they came from. God has put eternity in our hearts (see Ecclesiastes 3:11). But, the hardships of life and the thinking patterns of this world distort and distract us from that reality. What can be known of God is truly innate within us all! Therefore, we can appeal to the hearts of people regarding the truth that is in them (see Romans 1:19 KJV). It's not a truth about judgment, but a truth about origin—an origin found in the loving Father of all of the families of the earth (see Ephesians 3:15).

When people come to the knowledge of the truth and are

awakened to this reality, that *metanoia moment* is what evangelicals have come to know as being "born again." But I like to think of this as *switching the lights on* — or taking the blinders away (see Colossians 1:13 and 2 Corinthians 4:4).

Do I believe in a new birth? Yes, of course. But, you didn't **believe yourself** into the new birth, **Christ did**. Believing in Jesus' work did not *birth* you into the kingdom of God just like *believing* in your mothers ability to *"push!"* didn't *birth* you into this world. The work being done during the birthing process has absolutely nothing to do with the individual being born and everything to do with the one giving birth.

Jesus did the work; humanity gets the benefit.

Your belief doesn't birth you. Your belief recognizes that birth.

His resurrection was your rebirth.

"Blessed be the God and Father of our Lord Jesus Christ, who according to His great mercy has caused us to be born again to a living hope through the resurrection of Jesus Christ from the dead." 1 Peter 1:3 (NASB)

T.F. Torrance was once asked when he was "born again." Answering this question he said, *"when Jesus Christ was born of the Virgin Mary and rose again from the virgin tomb, the first-born from the dead."* [7]

When a man is awakened to this truth, He finally sees reality for the first time. He finally wakes up to what Christ has done on his behalf. He finally sees himself in Christ for the first time — his life hidden with Christ in God (see Colossians 3:3).[8]

---

[7] Habets, M. 2008. The Doctrine of Election in Evangelical Calvinism: T. F. Torrance as a Case Study. *Irish Theological Quarterly*, vol 73. pp. 334-354.

Is it necessary to *believe* this truth? Well, of course! Without this *change of mind* we will not experience the reality of what Christ has done. Sure, God is with us even in our unbelief, but we remain against Him and far from Him in our own minds (see Colossians 1:21) — blinded to the reality of His goodness and love — and thus living life with the negative effects of unbelief.

The reality is this: You are loved! You are accepted! Right now. Right where you are. You didn't have to do anything in order to please God or get on His *nice list.*

It seems that God cared about us when we didn't care about Him. It seems that God loved us all while we were still against having a relationship with Him. (see Romans 5:8)

You may have heard that God is angry with unbelievers and against them until they turn and believe in Him. But if we believe God is against humanity, then we will come up with strange ideas about God and create a dichotomy between the Father and the Son. Eventually we must conclude that God was angry at mankind and wanted to kill us. And instead of killing us, *God killed Jesus, His Son,* in our place.

So, *the angry Dad in the sky* took out His anger on Jesus so He wouldn't have to destroy us. And somehow, folks who believe this still say they believe that God *is Jesus* and Jesus *is God,* etc., etc. This belief is very normal in the foundation of Western

---

[8] I realize that I am touching a "holy grail" of sorts for believers, but we must think critically in regards to doctrine and be willing to change our thinking when a more biblical view is presented. We cannot lean on our *experience* to form our doctrine on the new birth, rather we must let Scripture define it. John Crowder and Francois Du Toit have done a marvelous job writing about the new birth. See John's book "Cosmos Reborn" and Francois' book "Divine Embrace."

Christianity but is detrimental to our understanding of the Father.

This idea is rooted in what has been popularly called **Penal Substitution**. I won't go into this here, but I'll mention a few thoughts that will hopefully change our thinking about the Father and His everlasting love for us.

The question is this: where was God and what was He feeling during Christ's death? Was He angry at humanity and taking it out on His Son? Was He giving Jesus a cosmic killing on behalf of the people that He desired to torture? Was it about justice? Did *justice* demand that God violently *kill* someone?

Paul gives the clearest answer to the question of God's whereabouts and feelings during the crucifixion in 2 Corinthians 5:19 when He declares,

" *God was in Christ reconciling the world to Himself, not counting their trespasses against them." (See 2 Corinthians 5:18)*

Wow! Did he just say what I think he said? Paul, are you saying that God was **in Jesus** during His time on the cross?

*"Yes, Blaise. That is what I am saying." ~Paul *sarcasm intended*

God was not abandoning His Son on the cross (John 8:28-29, John 16:32).

God never abandoned Jesus and God will never abandon you.

Jesus was quoting Psalm 22:1 when He shouted, *"My God, My God, why have you forsaken me?"* But every good Jewish boy knows that when you quote part of the Psalm, you have to take it in context. The Psalm comes to a conclusion in verse 24 with a wonderful declaration of God's continued commitment to His Son even while He was on the Cross.

*"For He has **NOT despised** nor abhorred the affliction of the afflicted;*

NOR has He hidden His face from him; But when he cried to Him for help, He heard."

Did God abandon Jesus? Did He forsake the Son?

No.

When Jesus *became sin,* He became our sense of shame and abandonment. He became the cry of the orphan, the widow, the slave, the lonely, and the agnostic who says, "God, who are you? And where are you?"

The answer?

He is **LOVE.**

He is **HERE.**

He is **NOW.**

In the midst of your **pain**. In the middle of your worst **sin**.

God. is. here.

Death and loneliness didn't get the last word with Jesus, and they don't get the last word with you.

You are not alone and you will

never

be

alone.

God didn't kill Jesus. And God will never kill you.

Man killed Jesus, but God raised Him from the dead (Acts 2:23-24). Jesus is God being killed **by us**, dying **for us**, and taking on the full identification of **our sin** that He might transfer the very identification of His righteousness **to us**—and all of this completely apart from **our permission or ability!**

Therefore, we can without wavering, simply declare to every person in existence:

"GOD IS FOR YOU!"

This word awakens faith through the hearing of the word of reconciliation (Romans 10:17, 2 Corinthians 5:19-21) and brings life transformation as it is received with simple trust!

When we see that God loves people in their deepest and darkest places of depravity and even when they are in opposition to Him, then we can do the same for them. We love others the way we believe God loves us. We view others the way we believe God views them. Do you see an angry Father, or do you see a loving and longing Father?

Is this the Father we see?

Is this the One we fix our internal eyes upon?

Do we see the God who never gives up and never let's go—the Papa who loves the lowest and most dysfunctional of His prodigals—to the end and beyond? If not, then let's take a fresh look and maybe we'll be surprised by what we find.

Immerse yourself in this message of love.

Drink deeply of the good news of the good God.

Find your identity in the face of Jesus—in the smile of the Father.

He is proud of you. He is for you.

Whether you know it or not, believe it or not, feel it or not, or even care at all... Jesus Christ is with you, near you, in you, and all around you.

YOU CANNOT ESCAPE FROM HIS HAND.

YOU CANNOT ESCAPE FROM HIS LOVE.

And you don't have to be a preacher or a missionary in order to experience the reality of His love. It is available to everyone. It's there whether you know it or not, but He invites you to experience and enjoy its reality constantly through *simple faith and trust.*

With the simple whisper, *"Jesus, I trust You,"* comes the flood of peace and joy in which contentment and fulfillment drowns itself and beckons you to join her.

Feel free to smile. Enjoy life. And talk to God every day. Knowing that He actually listens.

Cast your cares on Him because He really does care for you.

Trust Him with your heart and trust Him with your life.

Talk to Him about your desires and your plans.

Ask Him for help in the day to day, and ask Him for help fulfilling the dreams and plans He's put inside of you.

When hard times hit, they are a reason to rejoice because you know your life is not defined by circumstances but by a greater reality that has overtaken your very existence.

Christ is in you. God is with you. You are forever secure in His hand, and absolutely **nothing** can separate you from His **love**.

ABOUT THE AUTHOR

 Blaise has been preaching at churches and conferences for the last 14 years seeing the power of God's love awaken hearts and change lives. His passion is to preach Christ-crucified, sharing the gospel of grace that transforms lives and awakens people to their identity as children of God.

Blaise has a B.A. in Religion from Liberty University. He taught at Teen Mania Ministries Bible School from 2004-2008 and at the International House of Prayer Bible School from 2010-2011. He is also a professor at Radical Grace Online Seminary based in Houston, TX.

Currently, he resides in Nashville, TN where he writes, creates media, and travels as an itinerate minister.

Blaise Foret, Inc.
500 5th Avenue N. Apt. 107
Nashville, TN 37219
www.blaiseforet.com

9770212R00096

Made in the USA
San Bernardino, CA
27 March 2014